Praise for MD Marcus

"It takes courage to face our own deepest wounds, to look pain and loss right in the eye and refuse to blink. Perhaps more courage than most of us ever muster. And yet, in her debut book, MD Marcus does exactly this. In what proves to be as much a poignant, poetry-laced memoir as it is a permission slip for the rest of us to disbelieve our worst circumstances are the last word, Marcus is never glossing—and never without hope."

— Steve Daugherty, author of *Experiments in Honesty*

"MD Marcus' unflinching memoir bravely examines the intersection between depression, single parenthood, anxiety and grief, culminating in a beautiful story of loss, and love."

— Cinthia Ritchie, author of *Malnourished: A Memoir of Sisterhood and Hunger* and *Dolls Behaving Badly*

"This memoir is a brilliant balancing act of storytelling. Not only does it balance time, it balances prose and poetics, openness and control, and the reciprocal relationship between writer and reader. The writing moves with an honest intentionality. It is not a giving over of a narrative. It is a welcoming into a space we get to be exposed to but that is still undoubtedly the writer's. We are grateful for the invitation and thankful for what we gain from the experience. We leave excitedly waiting to be invited back again sometime soon."

— Dasan Ahanu, author of *Freedom Papers, Everything Worth Fighting For: an exploration of being Black in America*, and *Shackled Freedom*

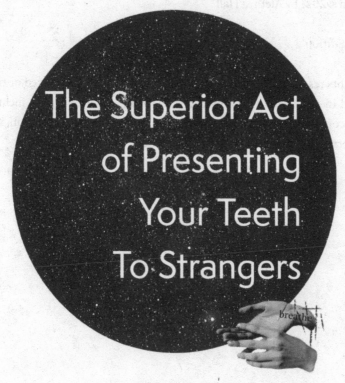

The Superior Act of Presenting Your Teeth To Strangers

a memoir

by MD Marcus

edited by Ericka M. Arcadia & Lance Umenhofer
design and illustration by Alethea Hall

APRIL GLOAMING

Publisher's Cataloguing-in-Publication Data

Marcus, MD
    The superior act of presenting your teeth to strangers / written by MD
    Marcus / designed by Alethea Hall
ISBN: 978-1-953932-02-0

I. Memoir I. Title II. Author

Library of Congress Control Number: 2020952473

Names have been changed.
Some have been omitted.
All else is true.

This book is in honor of my beloved sister,
Paula.
And is dedicated to her three little birds—
Skyler, Trey, Maggie
and to mine—
Jazlyn, Jack, Zipporah

I guess if I'm gonna bother to tell it, I'm gonna have to be honest. The truth hurts. And not just in the way where you make a hurtful observation about someone else and pass it off as "just telling the truth." But it hurts the most when you finally admit some things to yourself. Some things that maybe you've never said out loud or have never even acknowledged within the secure confines of your own head.

The caveat being that isn't it always the case with any first-person narrative that said narrator is adamantly, yet always inevitably, fraudulently earnest? I can swear to tell the truth, the whole truth, and nothing but the truth, so help me God, but it would only ever be the truth as I've seen it. With that unfortunate reality out in the open, this is the point where I am gonna start telling some truths, and I can only hope they get more honest, despite myself, as the story goes along.

The problem is, and always has been, that I don't know where to begin. It'd be pointless to start at my birth and go about making things up from there. My earliest memory at three years old wetting myself in a pool of primary colored plastic balls in Showbiz would be just as useless. So, I'll just start somewhere in the middle. I suspect that'll be as good a place as any.

part 1

How does anyone do it? How do they deal with life? My mind kept floating back to the same two unremarkable questions. I must have verbalized the query bouncing off the walls of my head because my therapist returned my question in the low, soothing tone that I am convinced must be taught in a prerequisite course at therapy school.

"Well, you've been through some pretty serious things in your life. How have you dealt with it?"

"Badly," I mumbled with a chuckle meant to be dismissive, but therapists are trained to see right through these sorts of mechanisms.

Avoiding the discomfort of her steady gaze, my eyes floated freely to the windows above her head. Three square windows in a row. She was the one who taught me squares can be a useful tool during the onset of a panic attack. You follow the outline of the square with your eyes, counting to four as you go, and then repeat and repeat. One, up. Two, across left. Three, down. Four, across right. Repeat. Supposedly, your mind can't count and go crazy at the same time. I still catch myself arbitrarily seeking out squares from time to time.

These particular sanity-saving squares happened to be just above ground level and looked out into the parking lot. Her office was in the basement of a rather large brick building, and I could see landscapers in neon-orange jumpsuits throw bales of hay off a pickup truck. I wondered how much they were paid. I know I would hate to work outside all day in this disgusting humid weather.

"Do you find it hard to stay present?" Her serene probing brought me back inside her office.

"Yeah, I guess."

This was not my first time in therapy, but I am never ready for these questions meant to inflict serious self-reflection. I've been to a therapist (or therapists, rather) more times than I'd care to admit, probably not as many times as I've actually needed. I've never found them particularly helpful. Still, for some reason, I have determined their council to be crucial to the process of my becoming normal, and I force myself to go from time to time. I wonder, had I seen a therapist earlier in life, if things might have turned out a bit different. But as a rule, I've found it's generally best not to stir-up "what-ifs." They tend to lead me down a road I'm certain to regret having traveled.

The thing is, I don't even like talking to people, so answering these questions already designed to make you uncomfortable is torturous in more ways than they're probably meant to be. I guess I shouldn't include all people in that statement. Just most of them. This hasn't always been the case, and try as I might, I can never quite pinpoint when this debilitating introversion occurred.

Bringing me back to the reason for my current torture session, my therapist went on, "You have some pretty good reasons to be depressed."

Maybe it shouldn't have, but this statement made me laugh, out loud and really hard. I never thought about seeking out validation for having gone crazy. But there I was getting reassured that I had every right to be.

Attempting to reel the session back in again, she went further to say, "You have some great inner resources. You have to learn to trust that about yourself."

At this point, I considered looking into her credentials. Trusting myself seemed like the worst possible advice. *Myself* hasn't always been extremely reliable, and it certainly hasn't led me to any successful outcomes heretofore.

Even now, all these years later, my mind still betrays me. At times, I can't even determine whether I'm in utter ecstasy or utter despair. It's like only a fine line exists where chasms ought to be. This was not always so, but not much for the better. The past found my Benedict Arnold of a mind still as traitorous as ever, but my darkness was opaque, and my joys registered clearly as momentary blips solely necessary for preservation purposes.

Struggling to gain my composure under her unmoving eyes, I could feel my face flush and my temper rise.

"I just don't want to be a crazy person anymore!"

"What does that mean to be 'crazy?'" She remained unmoved without any observable changes in expression through my laughter and subsequent frustration.

"To not be normal. To feel insane. *I am crazy*! I have crazy thoughts I can't control. I do crazy things. I have to take medicine to not think about killing myself. Normal people don't have to take crazy people pills. I go to hospitals for lunatics. These are the things crazy people do."

There are times when I actually do feel normal. Well, maybe a better way of putting it is that I am not conscious of feeling crazy; lack of crazy equals normal. This was just not one of those times.

"We don't like that word, 'crazy.' I want you to try and redirect your thoughts. Whenever you think to yourself, 'I am crazy,' stop that thought in its tracks and replace it with another thought."

Now *this* was going to be problematic. If you care to know, I'll tell you why, and I will let you be the judge of my sanity...

***

My Father's Flame

Sometimes I do not pray in the prescribed order. Instead I scrawl holy words over this sin-soaked flesh to quell what's beneath. Always seething, a hair's breadth. Paper thin, I did not eat the fruit. Yet, I was birthed naked under the sign of Fire. Written off. Excused. Without hope. Doused in blood, the sign of the cross pleads to extinguish this wicked birthmark, and again, an offering even to those born of alcoholic war veterans, born from inexorable rage. And you, dear one. Did I ignite the fire beneath your skin? Burn you to ash? Are you still alive?

Alive like me

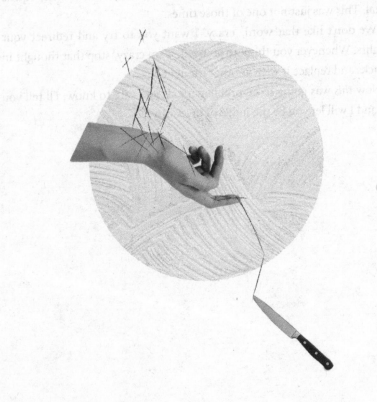

As you enter a mental hospital in which you are to be momentarily committed, reality melts into a puddle, resembling something akin to a slushy Monet collecting messily around your ankles. I found myself in my own Bedlam wading through my drippy life portrait consumed by sheer internal panic. If crazy has a smell, it would definitely be that of urine.

It wasn't the same as I remembered. The adolescent section must have been in a different wing of the hospital, or it could have just been that the decade that I'd presently managed to press my way through gave way to unfamiliar changes at Madison Grove Hospital. I now realized that where I was before was probably supposed to be decorated to make the place more "kid friendly," if such a thing was even feasible. I was in the adult unit now and, quite frankly, scared shitless. I was led inside as the second set of double doors clinked ominously behind me, removing any idea of freedom. This was it. No way out. The sinking sensation of helplessness dashed with fleeting sensations of utter riotousness must be what prisoners experience. This was, after all, a prison for the mentally ill.

I was accompanied into the unit and abandoned without any direction. Up against the wall directly in front of me leaned a young guy who looked to be around the same age as me. The band he wore on his right wrist left no doubt that he was also a patient.

With an expression I assumed was meant to be charming and seductive, he began looking me up and down and said, "Hey baby, how you doing?"

This could not be real. I wanted to scream at this idiot, "I am in a mental hospital. HOW DO YOU THINK I'M DOING?" But instead, I just gathered my thoughts and my person and walked away to the other side of the room without a word. The inappropriateness of men never ceases to amaze me, and I guess you ain't been hit on to till you've been hit on in a crazy hospital.

Patients roamed about freely ("freely" may be a bad choice of words) all over the place. As I looked around, slowly soaking in my surroundings, I couldn't help but think to myself that these are *real* crazy people. I always believed myself to be more along the lines of a functioning crazy or temporarily crazy, if you will. Not these folks. They were the talk to yourself, stare inappropriately, walk in circles, hard-core anti-psychotics needing crazies. Did I mention I was scared shitless?

The first patient who I couldn't help but take notice of was a man who reminded me of a deranged looking Jeff Daniels. The reason I couldn't help but notice Deranged Jeff (we'll call him DJ) is because he looked at me as if he'd like nothing more than to kill me on the spot. In this moment, I don't remember seeing anyone else, but try having someone glare at you with murder in their eyes, and you'd probably find it to be fairly distracting as well. If we had been anywhere other than here, I'd have given him a "What the hell you looking at?" scowl. As much as I'd like to think of myself as being intimidated by few people, even I'm not brave enough to stare unadulterated crazy in the face and foolishly dare it to do something.

Keeping DJ at a safe distance while managing to not ever make direct eye contact, I made my way over to an old, yellowed phone that was attached to the wall. It looked as if it belonged in 1989, but I desperately needed to talk to anyone who was sane enough to be on the outside of those walls. I picked it up and prayed it still worked.

Dialing my brother Lance's number, I wondered how much he already knew. I had been able to call one of my sisters frantically from the intake room hours before I was told I was going to be admitted, and she took it upon herself to inform my mother of the situation. That really pissed me off.

"Hello?" My brother answered the phone in a more question form than a statement.

"It's me."

"So, what happened? What's going on?"

"Well, I'm here, ya know? I've just been feeling like I was going crazy again, like on the verge of full-blown depression, and I didn't want to. I was trying to stop it. I wanted to do the right thing and get some help before things got too bad. Before it got even worse. But when I came here, they told me I had to stay. And they keep saying I wanted to run my car into a tree, and I didn't say that!" I stopped here because my volume was increasing and drawing attention just as I ran out of breath.

"Okay well, just calm down. I talked to mom and she's really worried. She's making calls to the hospital to try to get you out."

"Great. I didn't even want her to know I was here again! It's horrible here! There are literally crazy people *everywhere*," this last part I whispered into the receiver for my own safety. "They're just walking around next to me. I'm freaking out!"

"Just try and go to sleep, so it will be over quicker and tomorrow will come. It'll be just like Christmas," Lance responded with his usual quick wit and slightly inappropriate humor.

I could appreciate the comicality even within the situation, but I still wasn't able to muster an audible laugh. Getting off the phone, I wondered what I was supposed to do now. I had no interest in joining the crowd on the couch gathered around a small TV any more than I wanted to join the people sitting at a long table in the middle of the common area having an undeclared staring contest. I decided that to find my room would be best.

Just beyond the common area and the nurses' station to the left, there was a long corridor full of doors. My room was the first door on the right. Inside the room, I found two beds, a small bathroom, and not much else.

"What's your name?" asked an older woman sitting on the edge of the bed closest to the door. She had long gray dreads that were well grown out and in serious need of some attention.

Answering and then countering the question, I found out my roommate was named Betty. She appeared nice enough, and I didn't fear for my life, so things were looking ever so slightly up.

"We'd better get going," she said with each word drawn out as long as possible. She talked as if every word took all her concentration to form, and she applied strange inflections throughout her sentences that only served to confuse their meaning. "Group is going to start soon." And with that, she walked out the door.

Wonderful, I thought. All I wanted to do right then was hide out until my time there was up. I don't even like being in groups of sane people, and without knowing exactly what to expect, I knew this would not be anything I was going to like.

"Group" was held on the opposite side of the nurses' station from the TV and phone area. It was in a big, wide-open space with lots of chairs that formed a large circle. There were white boards on the back wall and an open door leading to a small room that I couldn't see into. Without any ceremony or instructions, we all quietly took our seats.

As I would soon discover, this was only one of infinite group meetings held throughout the day. In fact, every couple of hours there was a different form of "group." This group meeting was for goals, but shortly following would be group meeting for artistic outlet, group meeting with the psychiatrist, group meetings to count each other's toes, and so on and so forth. Since the outlawing of lobotomies and the taboo of electric shock therapy, I suppose mental facilities needed to come up with new, more acceptable forms of torture for the mentally ill. I found out quickly that "group" is what they're calling it nowadays.

This time, our meeting was led by Stephen. From his overly cheery disposition, I concluded Stephen couldn't have been working in the mental health field for too long.

"Right now, we are going to go around the circle and say out loud what each of our goals are for the day," Stephen announced.

As I began to mentally formulate a succinct speech that would make me appear sane and reasonable, while at the same time acknowledging my problems, Stephen called upon a man to his right named James. Up until this point, James was an unassuming guy sitting quietly to himself, but not creepily quiet.

"My goal?" James began. "Well, my goal is simple. To not catch a body up in here!"

I don't know if the fear and shock caused by this statement registered on my face, but I began retreating internally to a safe place. I'd have liked nothing better than to run out of the room screaming, but unfortunately, when you're in a place for the mentally insane, running and screaming is generally frowned upon. You must put on your sanest game face in the literal face of insanity, no matter the ludicrousness of the situations you're placed into, if freedom is to ever be restored.

James' psychopathic monologue continued, "Some people in here might think I'm gay or soft...or a sawed-off sucka! But I'm here to tell you differently because sometimes I feel like a nut...sometimes I don't."

Holy shit! was the only thought my brain could process.

Somehow, though, Stephen seemed satisfied enough with James' "goals" and moved on to my old friend, DJ.

Deranged Jeff declared with an air of being quite pleased with himself and his own cleverness, "I want to be a goaltender." At which, he laughed hysterically.

Next was a timid-looking lady named Missy. She was hardly audible and looked exactly how I felt. Missy's goal was to "just make it through the day."

Sitting to the right of Missy was Sylvia. Unlike the other patients who were wearing street clothes, Sylvia had on a blue hospital gown covered with neon cats. Her hair was shaved almost completely off, and she was immensely overweight.

After Sylvia murmured that her goal was to "do a puzzle," it was my turn.

Firstly, I hate talking to strangers, and secondly, I hate talking to large groups of strangers. While I'm at it, let me add that thirdly, I hate being in a mental hospital being asked to make public presentations about my personal goals to my fellow lunatics. That aside, I said some rubbish about taking my medication properly and going to therapy consistently in my most professional, not crazy, "let me the hell out of here" tone. After me, they moved on, and about seven others stated any manner of depressing or ridiculous goals.

We were released from this helpful exercise and allowed to go do as we pleased so long as it didn't include killing ourselves or each other. I walked to the nurses' station to collect my first round of medications. Even if you offered me a million bucks, I couldn't tell you what the hell they were giving me.

As I approached the desk, one of the nurses who had been looking down at some papers sat up abruptly and said to the nurse who was doling out the drugs, "Do you smell that? What is that smell?"

A patient who was standing next to the desk, whom I hadn't noticed from group, turned toward me with a look of revelation in her eyes and exclaimed, "I smell it too. It's buullsheeet!"

Saying a silent prayer that whatever these drugs might be, they would knock me the hell out, I gulped them down and walked straight back to my room. I was alone and grateful. Lying down, I hoped I could force myself to sleep for the remainder of the day. I closed my eyes and wished for morning.

Next thing I remember was seeing Betty sitting up on her bed and staring in my direction. She must have been watching me for a while, and I woke groggily under her steady gaze. I felt as if I did not possess enough energy to even control my limbs and sit up. The medication made me heavy and slow.

"Group is about to start. If you don't wanna come, then at least make sure to get some coloring pages," she said with those same ill-placed intonations.

The last thing in the world I cared anything about at that moment was getting my fair share of coloring pages. While Betty was offering her advice, there was a loud disturbance in the hall that woke me slightly more out of my drug-induced haze. A man's voice could be heard loudly and incoherently. I was mentally jolted awake but still felt the restraining physical effects of the drugs and couldn't move.

Betty must have picked up on my sudden alertness, and she explained that was just Thomas. Thomas was a tall, silent man I had unofficially met during the first group meeting. I remembered him immediately because he breathed like he was sleeping, and that bugged me. He gave the impression of being the type who would never cause intentional harm to any living creature. But it was the unintentional acts you had to be on guard for. He reminded me of Lennie from *Of Mice and Men.*

She explained to me that Thomas loves his brother, but his brother is starving him of attention.

"The less he gives him a shoulder to cry on, he'll get stronger. But if he's there for him all the time, then he stays weak. He can't sleep, so he roams the halls all day and night. They have to keep showing him back to his room. He has real problems...but I guess all of us here do..." Trailing off with this statement, Betty left the room.

I rolled back over, welcoming the sedatives' potency and fell almost immediately back to sleep. In what felt like mere seconds, I was woken up again. This time by a nurse who insisted I join in the next "group." I informed her that I was much too tired to attend a group meeting. With a gentle, yet stern tone, she replied that I had to go and that I would be able to get back to sleep right after the meeting was finished. For the life of me, I still cannot understand why they dish out drugs that are severely tranquilizing and then insist that you be functioning enough to go to meetings every freaking hour.

Dragging my semi-comatose body out of bed and down the hall to the meeting room, I could never have made up what they had in store this time. No more circle of chairs or statement of goals. Instead, there was gentle music coming from a radio that sat on top of a table and people milling about in various areas of the room. Just as Betty promised, there was a pile of individual coloring pages and a plastic Tupperware box full of crayons. James had managed not to catch a body yet and was dancing in a corner to the music. DJ, the "goaltender," was playing a game of checkers by himself.

23

Sylvia was sitting alone in a fold-out chair by the window, rocking back and forth. But overall, the majority of them were actually coloring.

I took a seat by myself and curled up in a chair. My plan was to discreetly go unnoticed until the hour was up and I could get back to the sweet escape of slumber. My plan unfortunately failed. I was forced to find something to participate in by the hippie-dippie art therapist who was wearing stupid round glasses and a skirt long enough to trip over. I figured that coloring was the only option in which I didn't have to engage with these people.

I'll tell you one thing right now, if you weren't before you walked through those double doors, coloring in a room full of grown ass adults who are all taking this shit seriously will damn sure make you crazy. I thumbed through the coloring sheets to find which I thought prettiest (hey, if I'm going to actually color at the age of twenty-seven, then it's going to at least be pretty). I picked a drawing of a cluster of flowers set in the middle of the page. What the hell? I decided I'd take it home (whenever it was that I went home) and save it in some sort of farcical scrapbook. *Grandkids gather round. Let ol' Grandma tell you about the times I went to the mental asylums. This here picture represents...*

Choosing just the right shade of blues and greens out of the big plastic crayon box, I took my sheet and my crayons to a long table and sat down as far away from everyone else as possible. Coloring slowly and carefully, I found myself listening to the music coming from the radio. It was no longer the therapeutic Muzak type, but a pop station playing a song I'd never heard before. It was actually pretty good, and it distracted me for a little over three minutes during that hell.

Dr. Hippie Dippie was across the room by the time the song was over, and I no longer had an adequate distraction. She was talking to DJ the way a mother talks to a toddler in a singsong voice, "So you're playing the game by yourself?"

Not even bothering to look up from the checkerboard, DJ said, "Yep. That way I can't lose." You can't really fault the guy's logic.

Right then, an old man named Otis came and sat down next to me just so he could stare out across the room at some unseen thing.

"Is it time for my meds yet?" he asked, and he kept asking anyone and everyone who would listen.

His eyes bulged out of his head, and he made repulsive noises with his mouth. Mouth noises are like nails on a chalkboard to me, and I cannot tolerate it. I had no qualms in moving rudely and directly away from that disgusting man.

I returned to my original individual seat near the windows where Sylvia was still rocking herself. Low murmurings were coming from her direction, and they began to get louder and louder.

"Ommm, chackel mum om ebego eebego, kill, kill...keeell!"

Wonderful. I decided to move seats again.

Luckily for me, shortly after I moved away from Sylvia and her rocking neon cats, group was announced over, and we were released from the room. I went back to the other side of the nurses' station to the phone. Trying my brother again, I got only his voicemail and went back to my room to give my plan at sleeping this nightmare off one more shot.

Not having been in there for five minutes, a chubby, young, bubbly girl came into my room to tell me I had a phone call. I got back up and beelined it past all the people meandering about to get to the phone.

"Who was that that answered the phone?" my brother asked.

"I don't know. It was one of the patients."

"What? They just let the crazy people answer the phone? Whoa. So, it's like the Crazy House Hotline?" He laughed, and he thought it was so funny that the next few times I spoke to him while I was there, he'd answer the phone, "Crazy House Hotline." I was not amused.

"Well, mom is calling everyone there trying to get you out. You should be happy she knows because she's not stopped calling around since you got there."

He probably had a point there. My mom may have been insensitive to my "mental" issues in the past, but she was also determined, persistent, and she made a habit of not taking no for an answer. She was certainly someone you'd like fighting on your side, *if* she's on your side, that is.

I can't really imagine how it must have been for my mom to have a daughter like me. For her, it was probably like trying to raise a unicorn. Not that I am some mythical winged horse or anything, but the circumstances were quite possibly nearly as odd for her. You wouldn't know what to feed a unicorn or how to really care for it since you'd have had no prior knowledge of unicorn life. So, my melancholy and tears surely weirded her out as much as if I had a solitary horn sticking out of the top of my head.

We were complete opposites on the emotional spectrum, she and I. I had always been fragile and sensitive, while I've never even seen a tear glisten in my mother's eyes. Not that she didn't have ample reason for them, mind you. When I first ran across the word "stoic" in school and subsequently learned the definition, I could readily think of one spot-on example.

My brother Lance told me that his wife, "Dr." Adams, had called the hospital and was given the head psychiatrist, Dr. Padgett's, home number. It's not exactly fair to put doctor in quotes because she is a real doctor, a resident at a teaching hospital a few states away, but I knew they took the liberty of making her come across a bit more official and made her out to be a person pertinent to the case of my sanity. Luckily for me, this gave my mom access to harass a higher up.

I've found that higher ups don't tend to enjoy being harassed. They're used to letting their underlings handle any disgruntled customers (or patients, in this particular situation). No matter how disgruntled they may be, the higher up wants the little guy to never give in while maintaining excellent customer service. Higher ups don't have the tact or the patience this requires, and they usually give in a lot more easily when directly confronted.

I'm not sure how we got off the phone, but I ended up sitting in the TV area much longer than I had intended. I started thinking how I'd like to walk around with no head for a while. In retrospect, I know that doesn't make any sense. But to hell with retrospect. Somehow the thought of walking about with no head seemed like it would offer some relief, and relief is what I needed.

A kind-looking, middle-aged nurse was suddenly standing over me, and she snapped me out of my gloomy reverie. She needed me to sign a stack of papers, some sort of consents I think. It may have been the drugs or the hopelessness, but I didn't even care to look them over. After I signed away my life and possibly my soul too, I began to embark on a restrained protest of my having been made to stay here in the first place.

"I really don't understand why I'm here. I don't think there's any reason I should be made to stay. All I did was try to be responsible and proactive. I know when I'm going crazy, and I'm not there yet. I am extremely familiar with my own signs and symptoms of depression. I've dealt with it since I was twelve. I am well aware of when I'm getting dangerously close and when I'm past the point of no return. I haven't even started cutting myself!"

Maybe I should have left that part out, but I continued, "I only came here because I needed help to not get too far gone. I just needed some resources. That was the right thing to do! I did the reasonable and sensible thing! That should not have made you all decide to lock me in here. I have kids. I need to go home. All I wanted was the names of some places I could go to get some medicine and start seeing someone. I do not deserve to be in here!"

"But you said you wanted to drive your car into a tree," the nurse replied with a gentle solemnness.

"I did not say that!"

My restraint was slightly wearing, but to my defense, what I really told the intake woman was that when I'm driving, a lot of the time I can't stop thinking about how I'd like to drive my car off a bridge. I did not have some fantastical "suicide plan" as everyone kept calling it to "run my car into a tree." I know this is not a great defense, and perhaps I was in no position to split hairs, but this difference made all the difference to me. In my mind, it was the difference between being crazy and not.

It's just that there's a monster living inside of my head. Maybe not literally, but sometimes it seems literal. I'm sane enough to know I don't actually have some green, three-eyed sci-fi creature creeping around the inner workings of my brain. But there's something in there that's very monster-like. Whatever this 'thing' is, I either try to keep it at bay, try to tame it, or just sit back helplessly while it takes over my mind.

When this demon takes control, it's all I can do to stay on the road while I drive. It tells me to turn my wheel in a direction that's counterproductive to living. And it tells me this a lot. The vast majority of the time, I'm not even suicidal when these urges enter my head, but the monster wants me to fatally crash my car nonetheless. It loves bridges, big trees, and those nice, large, yellowy-orange reflective square things on the ends of barricades along the sides of the road. As if I were a magpie, its glimmer transfixes me and calls me to it. When I see one coming, the monster speaks to me enticingly, at first saying, "Here! Right up here. See it? Go head, turn the wheel." As I ignore it, it grows increasingly aggressive; "Do it! Now, Goddamnit! TURN THE FUCKING WHEEL!" I grip the steering wheel tighter and talk out loud to myself with tears streaming down my face. "No, no, no, no! Not now!" I will stay on the road. I plead on. And so, the battle goes until I reach my destination.

The nurse went on, "I understand, but the thing is, everyone thinks of themselves dying, but not everyone actually says it out loud. The fact that you have major depression makes you more prone to act on these thoughts. There are many people dead who didn't mean to die, but the ambulance didn't get there in time. All they were doing was screaming for help. They didn't mean to end it altogether, but sometimes, that's what happens."

I understood her perfectly well but would not admit it. I know it's easy to make things really bad, real fast. You can have sex with someone in less than fifteen minutes and wind up pregnant or with an STD. These can be lifelong consequences. You can do drugs one time, become addicted, battle this addiction for decades, or you can die from it at any moment. You can commit homicide or suicide in a single instant.

Bad is easy, and bad can come really quick. Good is always much harder. Good takes forever. If you're broke, you can go to school and work your way up some up shitty ladder trying to dig yourself out of poverty's quicksand. But it sure ain't gonna come easy or overnight if you're playing by the rules. If you have a kid young, you'll probably be screwed for the foreseeable future no matter how many "good" decisions you make after that poor one. I wish it was just as easy to make things really good, real fast. Besides buying a winning lottery ticket, I can't think of any cases where good comes as speedily and efficiently as bad does.

I remained defiant and quiet as I thought about that phrase, "scream for help." I remember all the instances when I was told I was doing all this just because I wanted attention. It's ironic really, because I hate being the center of attention. It gives me tremendous anxiety. But even if all of it was just for attention, wouldn't it have been attention worth paying?

As a kid, maybe this opinion was the most hurtful part of it all. What I had wanted was to die, plain and simple. I was filled from my head to my toes with judgments of utter worthlessness. I saw the evidence everywhere. I hated myself for being worthless. I hated myself because I knew my worthlessness shone like a fluorescent neon light in the dark. Everyone else knew I was worthless, and that was completely humiliating. I felt there was only one sufficient option for me to rid myself of the hurt and to rid those I loved of the trouble my troubled existence caused.

Hate's a big word, and though I've used it frequently, it's fitting every time. I hated the thought of dying, but I hated the thought of having to live even more. And so, I started to cut myself. There were a few times I did this out of anguish in an actual attempt to die—a genuine effort to an end. But more often, it was simply to cause pain—to mutilate and to punish. From an outsider's perspective, I assume suicide makes more sense than cutting. Life gets hard, you get tired; you give up and off yourself. It follows a logical sort of flow. Suicide's more cut and dry (pardon the pun).

But the desire to cut yourself without the goal of suicide is harder to explain, and therefore, probably a lot harder to understand. The pain of cutting was a form of retribution for all my lack. I was still alive and didn't deserve to be. Knife. My body was the only thing I could exert some control over. Wrist. I cannot control these demonizing thoughts. Slash. They circle round and round and haunt and taunt. Blood. Physical pain replaces emotional pain. Relief.

Calling someone when these episodes arise makes you lose momentum. Too much time wasted on deciding who. Finding and dialing their number, more time. What words would you even use? Manufacturing a string of them to form sentences to make an outsider understand the pain within, a pain that at once provokes you and pleads to be destroyed is too lofty a goal. It's futile. Time better spent finding something sharp.

My body could never match the manic frenzy of my mind. Slow, deliberate steps to find the razor. My legs weighed a thousand pounds each, and I labored to use my body as a means to combat my mind. Move, goddamnit! I was like a thick mechanical robot.

I remember once, watching a movie with a man I was dating, where the main character was a girl slowly revealing herself to be schizophrenic. Mysterious bloody injuries materialized on her body without any explanation. My date wondered aloud, "What keeps happening to her?" Without turning my face away from the screen, I explained that the girl was doing it to herself. I could tell he thought he hadn't been paying attention to the part of the movie that must have exposed this, and he asked me, "How did you know that?" I told him it's obvious because of how constantly aware of her injuries she is. It was true, she was often in the mirror studying them or running her fingers over the bloody lines. He digested my answer silently and appeared to accept it without more questioning. But the second after I had given my answer, I feared I had also given myself away. In his silence, I heard him discovering my secret. Who could spot self-mutilation so keenly besides someone so intimately associated with it? I feared he spent the rest of the film watching, and at the same time, discovering my craziness paralleled with hers.

Since he called me the next day, I think maybe I was overreacting a little.

For me, the cycle of punishment in cutting became a habit whenever negative emotion began to rise and overtake my thoughts. It detracts. The habit then transforms into a coping mechanism. I'd bet the vast majority of people living with depression would be willing to take a certain level of physical pain over the mental distress they endure. And that, in my own weak and tiny nutshell, is the allure of cutting.

When things start to go dim in my head, even till this day, I know cutting myself would be the easiest way to relieve the emotional ambush. To not give into such temptation, I force myself into a mental showdown: me versus the knife. Most of the time nowadays, I win.

Coming to an impasse, the nurse and I both knew we weren't accomplishing much with one another, so we ended our discussion. It was no matter because it would have come to a quick end either way. Unsurprisingly it was time for, wait for it, another group meeting. This time we were being honored with the presence of an actual psychiatrist. The psychiatrists rarely show their faces to the patients of these mental facilities. They're more of "behind the scenes" type of operators, so this was a special treat.

Dr. Allen entered the group meeting room out of the door on the back wall that led to the mysterious unknown place. He was someone straight out of a 1990s movie, embodying everything the stereotypical psychiatrist was supposed to.

Shuffling into the room slightly hunchbacked, he was wearing a large, ill-fitting, burnt orange button-up sweater. An ensemble that no one who paid an ounce of attention to style or say, the TV, would have been caught dead in. The cartoonish combover that wispily fanned across the crown of his head was certainly laughable.

He began his presentation uninterested, which in turn, led him to be uninteresting. I don't know if he was married or not, but he was probably not the type of man who had an active social life. Even so, you could tell he wished he were anywhere but there with us.

Lecturing strictly to the white board and not even turning once to his half-conscious, half-coherent audience, he explained the differences in psychiatric disorders. His scattered circle doodles illustrated that I had non-psychotic major depression. This was a univocal thought disorder versus a mood disorder or bipolar. As it happened, I was a loser in life, but I had apparently won the mental disorder lottery. Next to a mild case of OCD, this was as about as good as it gets.

He confirmed the only voice in my head is my own. The thing is, though, my voice is just as dangerous. Just as deadly.

It was probably because my stint this time around was cut short, but I never did get to speak to Dr. Allen one-on-one. This was a marked difference from when I had been admitted here as a teenager. I spoke to the psychiatrist at least a few times during that stay.

He was a younger, supposedly cooler, doctor who I remember kept me on "checks" much longer than normal. Checks being a system of stringent suicide precautions where the patient wasn't allowed any potentially dangerous items. In addition, the patient is "checked" on every fifteen minutes to ensure they still had a pulse. The doctor prolonged my time on this system simply because I never asked for my shoelaces back. Seriously. All because I didn't ask for my shoelaces. I'll never forget the smug look on his face when he told me this reason. As if it were some profound and ancient Buddhist proverb meant for me to garner layers of deeper meaning, "You did not get your shoelaces back because you did not ask for them." And there I had been trying to be uncomplaining and not come across as insubordinate. In retrospect, it serves me right.

When, at last, Dr. Allen's presentation came to an end, I was finally allowed to go back to my room for the remainder of the night. The next day, I was released. There wasn't a great amount of fanfare, but the nurses and patients alike were all visibly surprised. I was told that not too many people get out after only one day. I was told this repeatedly during discharge and again after I had been released and had to muddle through outpatient mental health agencies. It must have been known that my family's incessant phone calls were the cause of my premature release because they all assumed I must have had a pretty "influential" family. Of course, I never admitted that the source of my fortunate turn was because someone at the hospital had accidentally given out a doctor's home phone number.

walls

murmurs of subversion
seep down
this geometric impound
plot to keep me awake
rob me of air
too deep to wade
    i drown
the silence reverberates
threatens to level
shelter and prison
bring it all down
solitude swells my head
till the weight becomes too much
rolls off my shoulders
i will not chase after
just let it abandon me
lying still my body
petitions the silence
for release
i sink into the mattress
deeper loss with every inch
my skin goes hot then cold
    the sun extinguished
never to return
darkness ever
evermore

It wasn't until five years after the first time I had experimented with cutting myself that I actually saw a therapist. I don't know how I convinced my mom it was necessary, but somehow, I had finally managed. Her annoyance was visible as she thumbed through the yellow pages to find someone who accepted our insurance. I was instructed to drive myself to the therapist directly after school for our introductory session the following day.

I might as well have skipped my classes that day because I didn't pay attention to anything the teachers were trying to get me to learn. Nervousness of having to meet a stranger and confess to her all my abnormal thoughts and feelings superseded anything that was going on. Luckily, her office wasn't far from my high school, or I may have chickened out before I reached it, went home, and pretended I had never made such an odd request in the first place.

Besides being my first therapy session, it was also my first time doing anything as grown up as going to an appointment by myself. After finding a parking space in front of the building with the same address that was written down in my notebook, I double-checked that the money for the co-payment my mom had given me was still in my backpack. As I touched the money, I felt like an idiot. My problems weren't even all that bad. I made good grades, and I never got into any trouble at school or with the law. I just couldn't stop myself from crying sometimes, and I had a frightening urge to hurt myself that was nearly uncontrollable. I got out of my car and walked in.

Moving toward the building was an out-of-body experience. I don't remember turning the knob, but there I was, standing inside the door. It opened directly to the waiting room, and I was the only person there. There was no receptionist or desk to check-in, just a few oversized chairs lining the walls with huge lime green pillows sitting on top of them.

There was an interior door that stood open directly across from the front door. Low music was coming from within, and I could hear the rustling of movement in the other room. I knew she was in there, and I also knew she must have heard me come in. There was no turning back.

A small white woman with dark curly hair that barely grazed her shoulders emerged. Holding out her thin hand, I met it with my own. It was cool and soft. She looked honest and friendly, and I instantly liked her. But liking her wasn't going to make it any easier to talk to her. I found it equally difficult to talk to strangers whom I had an affinity for as much as those who repelled me.

My first instinct was to smile wide and show my teeth. That's what I always did and often still do when I make contact with people I don't know. I probably do this with the intention of conveying the message, "I mean you no harm." I hope this will, in turn, disarm anyone who would wish to hurt me. My Crest strip bleached teeth serve as the white flag I wave throughout the day even when war isn't on the horizon. I surrender to people before I even say hello.

Smiling like a horse to someone whom I would be momentarily divulging my suicidal thoughts to felt stupid. I was a stupid smiling horse. But what else was I to do? To forcefully contour my face into a state of sadness that reflected my inner state of being was like acting. Pretending to be happy through my sadness felt more authentic than purposefully putting my sadness on display. So, a stupid smiling horse I remained.

I worried about what I would say to her now and in all the future sessions I'd imagined we'd be having. Of course, I couldn't have known then that this would be the last time I'd ever see her.

She shepherded me into her office in the kind welcoming manner of all genuinely nice people. This space was bigger than the waiting area and much more beautiful. It was done up in a contemporary design with plants in sleek pots, decorative metal wall hangings, and there was an entire corner of the room filled with children's toys. This area was safe. It was a place of life, not death, and she was the keeper of this life. The room took me

36

inside of it, and the comfort it offered made me stop paying attention to my posture. With slouched shoulders, I sat down and received everything that was being offered to me.

Having made introductions in the waiting room, she went about talking to me like a normal person. Maybe it was because I was seventeen and still technically a child, but every other therapist I've ever been to starts off with some version of the question, "What brings you in today?" I can't handle this type of manipulative prying as an adult, so it's understandable they don't bother expecting it from children. She talked to me in a way that made me want to share with her. I wanted to tell her things.

As I began trying to make sense of my feelings, my voice came out weak and dumb, as usual. I tried to make it relaxed, steady, and clear. It ended up just sounding cacophonous and weird. She didn't even flinch, and I started to love her for it.

I'm not sure how my ramblings led us here, but somehow as our conversation progressed, I began telling the story of how I had recently killed a cat. Right now, you may be ticking off your fingers, thinking "trifecta of a serial killer," but this incident was in no way intentional. It all happened when I was driving to drop my friend off to her house. We were cutting through the side streets of an unfamiliar neighborhood when out of absolutely nowhere, this little cat came running out. I gripped the steering wheel tight and swerved the car to avoid hitting it, but at the same time, the cat hesitated. Unfortunately, it then made the fatal decision to panic and dart back across the street. At the exact same time, my wheels were rolling over that exact same patch of asphalt.

The thump under my wheels sent a chill through me that I will never forget. My friend and I began a ghastly chorus of screams as I looked in the rearview mirror just in time to see its poor little body fly up in the air and smack back down on the street. It was awful.

All I could think about was how little Susie would soon come looking for Fluffy. I could not let her stumble across his mangled remains. I backed my car up, and we got out.

Using a shoebox and some napkins I had in my car, we collected the cat's body, wrapped it as best we could, and put it in the trunk. Driving to the first veterinarian's office we could find, we offered some concocted story of how we just "came across" this dead cat and wanted to bring it in. The lie was lame, but I couldn't handle the animal-loving workers looking at me with judgment and loathing in their eyes. That cat's death still haunts me.

Instead of offering analysis or assessment, my therapist shared a story about how she once ran over a turtle. The memory of the sound the shell made crunching beneath her tires made her shudder. Man, I loved her.

As it goes, all good things come to an end, and leaving from her office offered a taste of relief. I had revealed, at least indirectly, the heaviness in my mind. While the burden was still solely mine to shoulder, letting someone else know it existed made it rest a bit more squarely.

However, the relief was only temporary. Night always comes too quickly, and just as quick, the darkness leapt out of the evening air and back into my head.

Nights are as endless as the ocean on the horizon. The silence mocks. The fear weighs heavily, engulfing and tangling my mind. Rational thoughts disintegrate the moment they are birthed like a communion wafer as it touches the tongue. Now is the hour of crazy. There is no other soul awake in the world. There is no one else alive for that matter. I am all alone. Dark, quiet, haunting, nothingness, deserted hopelessness stretching until eternity. I am alone, lone, lone, lone.

The sobbing came again in crashing waves, and I heaved from its force by screaming into my pillow to muffle the sound. I didn't want anyone in the house to hear me crying, but my sorrow was too great to be confined within my body. Out it came.

God, I wanted to hurt myself just to quiet my mind because I could not stop this damned crying. I opened the top drawer of my nightstand and dug around until I touched the thin, cool metal of the knife I kept hidden away for moments like this. Gripping the handle so tightly in my left hand, my nails dug into my palm, leaving four tiny crescent-shaped impressions.

Placing the blade flat against my right wrist at first, I pushed down and opened my flesh. I moved the knife up and down like a see-saw, the blood oozing slowly and making a thin crimson line. As it began to collect and grow denser, it trickled down my arm like a soothing balm. I repeated this over and over, making three more lines.

After a while, my mom discovered me and called the therapist I had met earlier that day. While she explained to her that I liked attention and how I used to fake sick to stay home from school all the time, my therapist told her in no uncertain terms that she needed to take me to the hospital immediately. And that was how I wound up staying at Madison Grove the first time.

***

Vultures

stinking
rotting
carcass

discarded
disregarded

swarming until
life's departed

descending
unrelenting

picking away
decaying remains
juicy vitals
splattered stains

identity unknown

the bloodless heap
will no longer atone

spirit
long surrendered

nothing left
but a few
gnawed bones

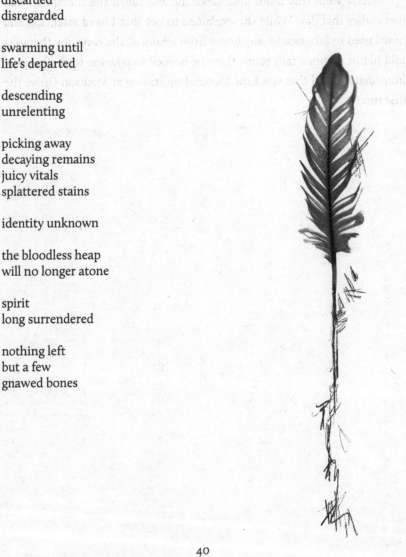

To enter the hospital, you must walk through a double set of glass doors. Upon going through the first set, you are required to wait in a glass box until the receptionist sitting across the room behind more glass presses a button on her desk that unlocks the second set of doors. You'll understand this security precaution is more essential from the reverse side of that door. Ensuring that if a crazy manages to get through the labyrinth of the hospital and out of all the other locked doors and somehow finds her way down to the first-floor lobby, there is still one last barrier protecting the public from her.

Obviously, my mom had to take me on this trip. I was a minor, and her presence and consent would be needed. The drive and wait in the lobby were as uncomfortable as an extra medium wool sweater. But we both did what we had to, signed in, and then sat waiting until an Intake Specialist would see us.

These intake people are tricky. I had no idea then, but I know now that it's best not to be completely honest with them. I used to think it was counterproductive to not have full disclosure about your mental health, but it's too dangerous to be absolutely honest or forthcoming. This makes their job much too easy. The intake person was responsible for writing that big fat lie in my file that stated how I wanted to run my car into a tree when I came there looking for help the second time around. Just in case I hadn't been clear before, I never said this!

Anyway, back to my first rodeo, the main entrance, reception desk, and waiting area were all in one small section off a short hallway full of doors on either side. Whatever rooms or offices lay within these doors must have all been tiny because the number of doors to hallway-length ratio made it seem quite impossible that all of them could actually have a working function.

We were called to enter one of these doors, and indeed the room was a tiny square. The tiny square contained a rectangular table filling most of the space. Surrounding the table were three burnt-orange vinyl and dark wooden chairs. There was a heft to their look that said they could not have been easily lifted. We took our seats, and with all things essential to the preservation of the human condition, began the paperwork.

Some questions were easy like, Do you find that you cry easily and often? Yes. Do you sleep more than normal? Yes. Do you hear voices? Um, No. Do you fantasize about hurting yourself or others? Myself, Yes. Others, No.

Other questions were slightly more complicated. Do you feel an overwhelming sense of guilt? Do you have difficulty falling and staying asleep? Have you had weight loss or changes in appetite? Hopelessness? Loss of interest? Hear or see things others do not? Feelings of worthlessness? Difficulty concentrating? Making decisions? Do you believe others are plotting against you? Have you considered suicide?

Unsurprisingly, there were enough yeses for me to be admitted.

After going back to the waiting room and sitting for a short period, I was collected to be escorted into the interior of the hospital. I discovered the admitting section was like the small mound of crumbly dirt atop an ant hill. All the real action was further inside. It took place deep within two solid wooden double doors. These two doors, the color of a number-two pencil, were the gateway to this nucleus. One side had a big metal bar across it that must be pushed for it to be opened. But a person's strength wasn't the only thing needed to enter. There was a small black plastic rectangle mounted to the wall next to the door that had the push bar. There was a credit card-like slot running vertically through it, and a small light shone a constant red at the top of it. Stop. Do Not Enter.

The sentry began to break apart. Like Charon silently ferrying toward Hades, they were opening to collect a new soul.

Though there weren't many people in the room, everyone who was there, including the receptionist, stopped and turned their heads toward the doors. They continued to swing open at the same time but in opposite directions. A man dressed in tan scrubs a couple sizes too big for him walked out and went down the hall. After gathering the necessary information and papers, he called my name.

My mom looked tired as she left the hospital. I wonder now how much she slept that night.

I walked to the man in the baggy scrubs, and he offered me a smile. I suppose it was meant to be a smile that told me not to worry, that everything would be okay. But instead, it told me he was tired and was just going through the motions. There was somewhere else he'd rather be than chaperoning crazy kids around this place, and it showed in the parentheses punctuating his lips.

Having swiped his badge through the credit card slot, the double doors ceremoniously opened again, beckoning me in. I would be going through them this time, and I'd have no way back out—at least not tonight.

The hallway through the doors was long and winding. I'd imagine it'd be really disorienting walking through these passages alone. There were many doors and elevators and adjacent hallways, none of which we took. The lights inside these doors were off because it was the middle of the night when people ought to be asleep, and the lights above our heads glowed a dim yellow, casting everything in a sickly haze. It could have easily been the setting for a scary movie, and I hated scary movies. After walking what felt like a half mile, we came to another elevator and went up to the third floor.

Stepping off the elevator, we entered a unit shaped like an ill-formed upper-case T. The line going across the top was proportional in either direction and consisted of patient bedrooms with each door wide open. A nurses' station sat where the line perpendicular to the horizontal top line should have begun to come down. But the vertical line shooting off from it was too squat and short to form a proper letter T. This severed, would-be line contained a room full of chairs, a couch, a love seat, a TV mounted high on the wall, and a large conference table.

Even through the gloomy lighting, the primary-colored painting above and around each doorway, which served as a border throughout the unit, could easily be made out. It was the same color scheme found in most daycares.

Like the rest of the hospital, the floors there consisted of large, plain, laminate tiles that captured the sound of footsteps and made them almost disappear. Unless of course you happened to drag your feet when you walked, then the noise was all squeaky like the screech of sneakers on the hardwoods of an indoor basketball court.

Without a word, my guide left me with the same distant smile with which he had received me. Perhaps now he would get to physically go wherever he had already been mentally.

The nurse who reviewed my intake forms went over some safety provisions with me. This is when I lost my shoelaces. When she was finished checking my pockets, she led me to a room two doors down from the central location of the nurses' station.

The inside looked like a cheap motel room but was considerably smaller. When you entered, there was a tiny bathroom immediately to your left. It was all white with no additional décor or coloring. There was a small sink, toilet, and shower/tub combo. The only thing worth noticing about this bathroom was that there was no mirror above the sink and no lock on the door.

Inside the room were two twin beds. In the bed nearest the door, a girl lay asleep. I didn't want to disturb her, less from the worry of interrupting her sleep and more because I had no desire to meet her or talk to her. Quietly, I went past her bed and sat atop the comforter of the second, which was nearest a large window looking onto the street where I entered the hospital. It's probably a safe assumption that the window contained a particularly reinforced type of glass.

Staring out of this window, I made a mental note to remember the tree that was directly below. It was a tall tree between the street sign and a small bush with tiny white blooms. It lined the street of the main entrance to the hospital. Hundreds of people must pass that tree every day and fail to notice it, but I would always see it. I promised myself that I would always give it a small internal recognition if I happened to pass by. It would serve as a sort of symbol or a personal monument. It would serve as a reminder of a time I vowed never to forget. Probably couldn't forget even if I tried.

Sometime between my making promises to trees and the sun rising, I had fallen asleep. Now, I was being wakened up much too early by an unfamiliar woman. She was standing over my bed and softly calling to me. It was time for breakfast and meds. All I wanted to do was go back to sleep. I didn't want to have to talk to anyone I didn't know. I didn't want to have to meet other crazy kids. I didn't want people staring at me.

I got up to use the bathroom and could think of only one thing. Facewash. Man, I wish I had my facewash. I despised the thick sheen of a dirty face. It made me uncomfortable like I was dirty all over. Now a greasy, stinky, shiny oil coated my skin like a layer of film atop a cooling soup. They didn't have any facewash there, so I had to use bar soap, which is horribly drying and counterproductive. But beggars can't be choosers, and the grease had to go. No makeup either; it wasn't allowed. Not that I wore much then, but I did like to fill in my asymmetric eyebrows, especially the left one with the triangle-shaped scar where hair no longer grew. This scar was a gift from a childhood friend who accidentally swung her green plastic National Geographic box hard (which held informational cards about various animals), landing right above my eye. I remember screaming, "I hate you!" as I ran bleeding inside my house.

Besides filling in my scar, I liked to wear mascara sometimes too, but there was nothing to be done about that now. I stepped out into the unit common area raw.

There was a line forming at the nurses' station. Three people were already queued up, and others were making their way. They were all teenagers, looking to be anywhere from thirteen to about seventeen years old like me. I didn't consider it then, but I was probably one of the oldest. I'm sure eighteen is when they send you to the other side of the hospital.

Standing behind a gawky-looking boy, whom I estimated to be a couple years younger than me, I got in line. I didn't even know what we were waiting for yet. I watched as the nurse handed a small cup to the girl in the front of the line. It was the type of tiny paper cup found next to the water dispensers in nail salons. They're the kind that are not big enough to hold an adequate amount of water to quench your thirst, unless you refill it about seven times, and you'd look ridiculous doing that. When I reached the nurse handing out these cups, I found that they were not filled with water or any other drink, but rather, with pills. She asked for my name and then put two pills into my cup. Others had more. A few had less. The nurse handed me another tiny cup filled with a quantity of water only sufficient for swallowing pills, and she kept her eyes on me as I choked them down. I had no idea what they were or what they were for, and no one ever told me either. We would line up like this every morning and every night. Some people had to come for medicine even more often than that.

Being brand new to the unit, I was on "checks" and wasn't allowed to go downstairs to the cafeteria for breakfast. Instead, it was brought up to the few of us who were confined to the unit, and we ate at the big table in the common room. The food was disgusting: eggs in the shape of a block, toast that tasted like paper, and a rubber sausage. I learned that first morning that I'd have to get acclimated to being hungry for a while.

From my morning observations during the med line up, there looked to be about six of us patients in this unit. There was an even larger number of staff who worked in various capacities to look after us. I hadn't bothered to take note of what positions each had, but what I did know was that some were around more than others. That was the crux of it all, really. The ones who stuck around more often were the ones who talked to us like we were real people and not simply a liability.

The doctors interacted with us the least, which is not a huge shock, but when you think of it in the terms that they were the ones responsible for deciding our medications, our treatments, and when we would be released, it just seemed wrong. They would see us for maybe fifteen minutes out of an entire day. But perhaps that's what all their years of school were for: to be able to spend as little time with their patients as possible and still make critical judgments on their behalves. The adults who spent the most time with us usually ushered us to and from different areas around the hospital and stayed there with us. We would talk to them, and they would listen, but then again, they probably were relatively undereducated, and therefore, didn't have any real power to make significant changes.

After breakfast, I experienced for the first time that funny little thing called "group." It wasn't so bad then. They seemed much more organic compared to the ones I would attend as an adult. But this morning's group was one of the only few that really stood out during my first stay. I'm sure we had more because we were always meeting for something, but this first one was what I'd envision an AA meeting would be like. Going around the group one by one, we stated our names and why we were there.

A sturdy-looking girl with brown hair piled on top of her head in a messy bun went first. She had a large bandage wrapped around her left wrist. Before she even opened her mouth, we all knew why she was here.

She had been brought by way of ambulance. After having been treated and stabilized at a local hospital in the town where she lived, she was taken to Madison Grove for further management of her "injury." Her cut was severe, and I sensed, beyond self-mutilation. I think she had actually tried to kill herself, but suicide was a bit like killing a cockroach. You must be deliberate and forceful enough the first time, or it's liable to get away, and you will miss your opportunity.

She didn't explain any whys. Only the facts, which she told in a voice not too loud or too soft. She wasn't apologizing for what she did, but she wasn't defending it either. I admired her.

The boy who stood in front of me in the medicine line went next. He was skinny with dirty blonde hair, and I assumed he played in his school's band. His instrument was probably the trumpet. Behavioral problems were his issues. I don't know what they were exactly because he was so vague. Being vague was purposeful, though. He blamed someone else for him being there, for his problems. Maybe it was his parents, or maybe he was bullied by kids older and cooler than him.

His pity party was annoying, but when he had finished talking, he started doing the most amazing hamboning on his thighs. Slapping his hands together and letting them hit his legs, one and then the other, with amazing rhythm and speed. His hands flew while the rest of him stayed still, which gave the impression that this required no exertion at all. He beat out a tune straight from a Bugs Bunny cartoon. It was the "William Tell Overture" by Gioachino Rossini.

Da da duh da da duh da da duhduhduh da da duh da da duh da da duhduhduh da da duh da da duh da da duhduhduh da da duhhhhh da da duhduhduh

Bump the trumpet. He was definitely a percussionist. From that that day forward, I practiced his art in my spare time until I gained good speed and decent proficiency. I would never do it in front of a crowd like this, though. I wasn't quite as brave as he, and even with all my practice through the years, his skill was still far superior to mine.

Group continued in this manner. My turn came and went, and to be truthful, I couldn't tell you what I said. I can only be for certain that I smiled through it and avoided eye contact. Maybe I said I was a cutter or loosely referenced depression. I might have even been honest and admitted that I wanted to die. I kind of doubt the latter, though.

There was one person from our group who scared me, but he was probably capable of frightening men twice my age and size. Most of us kids there were just terribly sad and felt alone. Some were even justifiably angry and defiant. But he was a whole other breed of volatility. He was a mountain of a boy who had the strength of a man scarcely confined just beneath his skin. The sparse words he shared were spat out of his mouth like chewing tobacco. He was plenty mad and not at all afraid to do something about it if need be. And who was there to operably challenge any of his logic or frustrations? If he did lash out, it would have probably taken all the staff on the entire floor to restrain him.

Group came to an end, and that first day went on in a hazy kind of way. That evening, after everyone was medicated and instructed to get some sleep, I lay on my twin bed in my double room all alone with my eyes closed. As luck would have it, my roommate had been discharged that morning, and I couldn't have been more grateful for that. I was physically exhausted and emotionally drained, but as usual, mentally wide awake. Thoughts swirled through my head, each one faster and faster as if trying to avoid being caught. Did I really need to be here? Why was I crazier than other people? How come they can handle life without wanting to die? It's cold in this room. What were my friends doing? Are people asking questions about me at school? Oh my God, does everyone know? Am I going to be really far behind on my classwork when I get back? Will I be able to catch up? I wonder what kind of locks they have on these windows. Are these stupid checks going to wake me up every fifteen minutes all night long?

Just when my mind was getting worn out by this cyclical exercise and sleep was within reach, the screaming began. Screams full of rage and fear. It was the sound of someone wanting to be physically free, but I could tell his screams only caused his restrainers to work harder. In between screams, I could hear the hushed, urgent talking of the adults. One of my peers had done something in the middle of the night that provoked them into using a four-point restraining device. Then out came the needle.

It was a male voice whose screams ranged from furious demands to hysterical pleading. It didn't take long for me to recognize that it was the angry boy from group earlier that morning. He must've saw the nurses produce the needle, and he was fighting fiercely against it. Like a cornered animal, he gave one last outcry before he was defeated and all went quiet.

I didn't go to sleep that night.

The next day started with the same routine. Everyone woke up way too early, lined up for meds, and then those off checks lined up again to go downstairs to the cafeteria for breakfast. The rest of us waited in the lounge area for our trays to come to us.

Next was group. Routine was essential here, and they obviously had one firmly established. After group, some of us broke off to meet with our psychiatrists. Mine was named Dr. George Clayton.

49

There were small rooms next to the elevators that you probably wouldn't even notice if you passed by them. Dreading the conversations to come, I was led to one of these rooms to be evaluated by the doctor. Looking back, Dr. Clayton probably wasn't all that old. Maybe mid to late thirties at the most, but through my seventeen-year-old eyes, he was an old man. He was an old man who wanted me to talk about uncomfortable things. He didn't care how shy or embarrassed I was. He just kept asking questions, no matter how ridiculous they were, and expected me to give him answers.

If one of the objectives in the manila file he kept making notes in was to resign myself to stupidity, well, mission accomplished. I just wanted to leave, but I knew better than to even try that. So, I sat there and tried to smile to show I was normal and compliant, and I suffered through it.

We sat at a small table that was way too close for comfort. He pulled out a pile of what looked like flashcards, but instead of having math problems or words to read, they had black inkblots on a white background.

"Tell me what you see."

A butterfly. A train. A light bulb. An upside-down house.

Easy enough, but what could possibly be the implications of my seemingly benign answers? Could seeing a light bulb where there was none indicate a propensity to harm animals? Was the butterfly an answer only a schizophrenic would come up with? I don't know. I really saw much of nothing, but they press you to answer in situations like these, so answers I gave.

Next, we moved on to the scenario pictures. These were large pictures of scenes printed onto letter-sized sheets of paper.

"Tell me what's going on here."

I wasn't ashamed to tell him I had no clue what on earth he was asking of me. I didn't realize I was to look at these pictures and make up a story about what was happening. I mean, that's weird. The first picture was inside of a house. There was a little girl at the bottom of the stairs, and she looked sad. No, disappointed; she looked disappointed. Going up the stairs was a little boy. I decided they were brother and sister. That seemed to be a safe enough assumption. The little girl was disappointed because her brother was getting to go somewhere fun, and she wasn't. He was going up the stairs to change clothes and to get ready to leave. I found this exercise extremely stupid and pointless.

After a few of these pictures, we moved on to him asking me a set of verbal scenario questions. For example: "If you found a letter on the street that was sealed, stamped, and addressed, what would you do?" Simple, I'd pick it up and put it in a mailbox. Isn't that what everyone would do? This couldn't have concluded quickly enough.

Dr. Clayton then asked me if I had any questions, and as a matter of fact, I did. I wanted to know when I was getting out. His answer was clinical, vague, and unsatisfactory. Then I asked the question I most regretted—why I wasn't off checks yet. He, in all his god-complex-like glory, beamed as he told me it was because I had not asked to be off yet and had not asked for my shoelaces back. He allowed a dense pause to let that sink in. According to him, most people would've asked much earlier, but now that I had asked the magic question and posed no foreseeable threat, I would be taken off immediately. Thus, my first session with the psychiatrist ended.

I left the room and the doctor, collected my shoelaces from the nurse, and as it happened, I got off checks just in time to go to "class." Madison Grove's version was nothing at all like real school. It started off by echoing most of our daily tasks during which we lined up and blindly followed the commands given. We could have been going to the cafeteria, to the gym, anywhere off the unit really, but this time we were going to their adaptation of an education. This simulated schooling happened only once during my stay, and once proved more than enough.

Following one another single file, we were supervised by two staff members. We outnumbered them about 4:1, but they were equipped with restraining mechanisms, and we were instilled with a fundamental level of fear that kept us from trying anything.

Down several floors, we found ourselves walking the halls of a cold, windowless basement. Our class was held in a small square room with three rows consisting of those uncomfortable chair/desk combinations. A chalkboard hung on the wall, blank all but for shadows of writings past. A clunky old tube TV was mounted above the chalkboard. There was a VCR attached. We were going to watch a video.

One of our babysitters left the classroom, and the other popped in the tape. I don't know what I expected to begin playing, but I know I did not expect for us to watch a talk show. Graphics and intro music from another decade came from the TV, and Phil Donahue was our host. Now, I'm old enough (or young enough, depending on how you look at it) to remember watching plenty of Phil Donahue shows. But at this point in time, it had been off the air for many years, and I couldn't guess what such a dated television show could have to offer a group of mental teenagers.

Were we supposed to take notes or write a paper? Did they even trust us with pencils? Probably not. If there had been an assignment, I would have remembered and probably would have asked if I was allowed to keep it. We all just sat quietly in that basement classroom and watched the show with various levels of attention.

The topic, naturally, was teen suicide.

There were young kids in some classically 80s-looking ensembles telling their stories and describing their symptoms. Their parents joined them, and Phil led the discussion, which must have been quite groundbreaking television at the time.

Then out came the parents of the kid who actually accomplished what he had set out to do. This was sad, of course. Did it make us consider our parents? How would they be able to withstand us dying at our own hands? Would they go on TV and cry and immortalize us through tales of how we were such good and kind children? Would they preach what they could have done to prevent this, and what you at home can do to keep this tragedy from happening to you?

The show ended, and before we went back to our floor, they let us go outside in a small bricked-in courtyard for ten minutes. When we stepped out, it was like seeing a group of vampires from a poorly acted B-movie. We all shielded our eyes and noticeably cringed one by one from the bright light of the sun, which most of us hadn't seen or felt firsthand in several days. As soon as our eyes became properly adjusted, it was time to go back upstairs.

Returning to the lounge area, I sat with some stragglers on the couch. The routine of the hospital had blanketed me in a sense of predictability and security. I didn't like it there, but at this point, I was just riding the wave and biding my time. But the following day something happened that would rock me, all the kids on my floor, as well as the staff, not to mention the nation, and possibly the entire world.

There had been a shooting at Columbine High School.

***

We had all finished eating lunch by the time the news reports started coming in, and they would keep coming in all day and all week. The horror of it all kept us frozen in our chairs as the haunting stories leapt out of the TV and into our consciousness forever. At first, we didn't know what to make of it. As more and more details came in, we knew it was really bad. Much worse than any school shooting we had ever heard about before. Two high school seniors walked into their school, killing twelve students, one teacher, and causing the injuries of twenty-four other students before killing themselves.

Questions swirled, and speculation flew. Who were these kids? Why did they do it? The media was full of theories: Trench Coat Mafia, bullying, violent video games, Goth, antidepressants, and on and on.

One thing was undeniable. The atmosphere in our unit changed. The shift in mood was almost tangible. The staff went from no nonsense, getting through the motions, yeah yeah okay mechanical mannerism to being shaken to the core. They were shocked and saddened. But more than that, I sensed they were afraid. As they sat together with us, all our eyes were fixed on the same spot, and it dawned on all of us as we watched. We were those kids. Not the victims, but the shooters. We were the depressives, the outcasts, the Goths, the psychopaths. We were bullied, sad, angry, in trouble with the law, and medicated. A realization was silently and collectively made. They weren't afraid of us, but rather afraid of the responsibility they knew they held. Suddenly, their serious occupations got much more serious. It was their job, in part, to make us whole before sending us back out there into the real world. What we saw on the television that day was the saddest kind of reminder of what is possible if that didn't happen.

In group, they expected us to talk about Columbine. What could any of us say? Processing the idea of these kids as heartless killers was too much. The thought of terrified children hunted down, tormented, and shot at by their classmates was too much. The thought of planning and executing such atrocities was too much.

It was the quietest session we would have during my time there. Even the usual people who liked too much the sound of their own voices were muted. The adults didn't force us, and we soon took our medicine then were sent to our respective rooms with those images and our thoughts to keep us company through that long, dark night.

※

The following day was the same as every other day with two exceptions, one being that I got to go to the cafeteria for breakfast for the first time. After the morning meds, those of us off checks got to line up near the elevators to go downstairs. I felt sorry for the poor suckers who had to stay on the floor with no shoelaces and nasty food.

We were all about as excited as a group of second graders going on a field trip, ecstatic to leave our unit. More than anything, the tiniest taste of freedom was more delicious than any meal they could have offered.

When we got to the first floor, I recognized that the cafeteria was near the set of double doors that led to the main lobby. The thought of being that close to the outside was a little bit unsettling. I visualized myself breaking away from the group in a full-out run toward those doors. I could see myself pushing my full weight against them until they gave way, and

I could run through that set of glass doors and get back to real life again. In my imagination, all of this could happen in less than a couple minutes. Rationally, I knew that there were many reasons why this would never have worked. For starters, our chaperone would probably yank me back and restrain me physically before I even touched those doors. Secondly, I knew no amount of weight I could exert would make them budge open. Next, if I were able to get them open, the secretary would make sure those glass doors to the outside remained securely locked and would just watch my futile attempts behind the safety of her glass box. Finally, if I did make it outside, I'm sure they would have sent a team of people after me to capture me and return me like a fugitive. Worst thought of all, an outburst like that would set me so far back, they'd probably keep me in here for ten more years.

So instead, I stayed quietly in line, and we went into the cafeteria where we slid down one by one past the tables of food and picked what we wanted to eat. There was a variety of pastries, though they all looked dry. You had your typical fruit servings: oranges, apples, bananas, and then some yellow blobs that resembled eggs. But what made up for all these mediocre offerings was the bacon. Bacon makes a lot of things better. So, I got as much bacon as they would allow, which was a lot, a piece of toast with one packet of butter and one packet of jelly, a banana, and a carton of white milk. Not too shabby for a loony bin breakfast.

The second event that made this day a little bit different than the others was that after our midmorning group session, we went to P.E. Their version of P.E. was probably a lot more like high school than the Phil Donahue classroom session had been.

Just like the cafeteria, the gym was located on the first floor of the hospital, and it looked exactly like my school's gym minus the bleachers. They brought out a bunch of basketballs and gave us the option to play ball or walk laps. These options and the selection process that ensued echoed many of my own high school gym experiences as well.

Having never been particularly athletic, I chose to walk the perimeter of the court and kill a little more time of my indefinite sentence. One of our staff escorts came and walked next to me. He was a big guy who looked like he could put just about anyone immediately in their place if the need arose. I don't know why he came to walk with me. Maybe he thought I was lonely.

He made some preliminary small talk, and for some reason, I wasn't as intimidated talking to this large man as I was with most adults or strangers. Though he was an authoritative figure, he never projected any bit of superiority or judgment. I can't say that if I was in his position (now or then), that I would have been able to do the same. Working all day with crazy kids, who most people would probably think just needed a swift kick in the pants to straighten them out, couldn't have been an easy place to practice the art of non-judgment.

Where there was no judgment, there was also no pity. He wasn't coddling either. Somehow, he just accepted my situation at face value, nothing more, and nothing less. Out of every occurrence I had while at the hospital, this was the one encounter that sticks out like a sore thumb. Not because it was most memorable, but just because it didn't really fit. Everything else was so negative or condescending or disingenuous medical attention or something else altogether. This was different. He cared though he had no reason too, and he cared without agenda. Though I felt at ease, I still scarcely had anything to say. I was comfortable walking without words for a while. Then he broke the silence and told me something that caused a shift on the inside of me. Something I'll never forget.

"You don't belong here. You are different than these other kids."

He went on, telling me he had never said that to any other patient, but I didn't need this reassurance. I could tell he meant what he said, and he fully believed it, and for some reason that I still can't comprehend, he fully believed in me.

I was different. I didn't belong there.

Though he knew I was sad (okay, sad would be a weak adjective here), he said he could tell I could make it through. *I was different.*

Our allotted time for physical activity was ending. My new friend needed to help wrap things up, so we could make our way back upstairs. Before he left my side, he told me one last thing.

"I never want you to come back here."

Even if he never did find out, I hate so much that I let him down.

*∗∗

Though it felt like time stood still while a year's worth of days and nights went by, I was only in the hospital for a grand total of one week. When my time was up, my mom came to take me home. Without much ceremony, I left Madison Grove with a prescription for Prozac and instructions to see a therapist. I took the pills for about two weeks after being discharged before I decided I was better and didn't need them anymore. I also didn't bother going to a therapist either. My mom didn't push the point. Of course, I would eventually go back again (to many therapists and the hospital) in the years to come.

*∗∗

a black friday

coldness reaches under
mounds of blankets
shaking me awake
to an unfamiliar hour
dressing amidst
cumbersome darkness
quilting together pieces
of protection
forming more layers
of worry
that it will never
be enough

my stomach whines
making pleas
disguised as promises
to God
vowing this time
will be the last
hurried by images
forming in my mind
of lines that wrap around
shiny buildings
with greater desperation
than hope

taking my place outside
amongst the smokers
and loud talkers
wedged between
questions and complaints
I watch little children hide
in and out of shifting legs

they ought to be in cozy beds
not shivering
ignored
their classmates won't

have been up since 4 am
won't have stood outside
in some wretched processional
may never blink open
their eyes
recognizing that they possess
the ignorance of childhood

but children of the poor
know mornings with no light
know the sharp edges
of seasons changing
know the potent demands
of hunger

scolded by weary women
they burst free
to invent new ways
of passing these dark hours
chasing each other
around an empty flagpole

Having been confined to illumination through artificial means for the past twenty-four hours, the sunlight hurt my eyes and made them water as I exited through the hospital's main entrance. I didn't come in with much, so all I had in my possession were my keyring and discharge papers from my second round at this place.

Maybe it was the medication that was still in my system, but I couldn't remember where I parked my car. I probably pulled into the parking lot in a frantic haste the day before, assuming I'd be in and out within an hour or two. It was as if mini lifetimes had gone by while I had spent the intermediate time panicking over my safety and indefinite loss of freedom.

Wandering around for a while in no particular hurry, I eventually located my car in a lot next to a row of trailers. They couldn't have possibly been erected in less than a day, but I had no recollection of ever having seen them before, and looking at them now, I wondered what on earth they could've possibly been used for.

My car was old and used like every other car I've ever owned. There was a big dent in the driver's side door, and it opened only about halfway before I had to put some weight into it. Jerking it harder, the door came fully open. This physical exertion compounded with my mental fatigue made me want to just be still for a moment. The sunlight and heat that had entered the car over the past day made it stiflingly warm inside. I didn't have the energy yet to start the car or roll down the window, so I just sat in the heat with the door shut behind me and started thinking.

Discharging from the hospital was as frightening as having been admitted in the first place. Don't get me wrong, I was thrilled to be able to leave. But no matter how much I had fought it, I knew I really did belong there (maybe not coloring pictures), but I belonged there just the same. Being left alone, having to make decisions, taking care of my children and myself, in addition to the requirement of not having thoughts about directing my steering wheel away from the road was too much right now. When the nurse talked me through my discharge, I pretended that I would be okay, and so that's what was expected of me. In reality, I knew it was not completely safe for me to be left alone in this state, but I had no other choice. I had kids who had no one to watch them except for me. I was all they had. Right now, you're probably thinking *poor kids*, and you would be exactly right.

In a daze of doped-up exhaustion, I finally started the car, and in my zombie-like condition, miraculously succeeded in driving myself home. I also managed to resist the many opportunities to crash my car into the dozens of trees I passed en route.

Pulling into the parking space directly in front of my unit, I hurried to grab my purse, keys, and papers. I wanted to get out of the sunlight and out of the open where someone might see me. I hadn't looked into a proper mirror in a matter of days and hadn't had the tools to correct what I saw anyway, so there was no telling what physical state I was in. I fumbled a bit with my keys, but it didn't take too much time to unlock both the deadlock and the bottom lock. I turned the knob, shuffled in quickly, and closed the door as fast as I could behind me.

My apartment was dark and disgusting. Exactly the way I had left it. Opening the door, the smell of some rotten food or lingering garbage greeted me. Climbing carefully over piles of clothing, trash, and toys, I made my way through the living room. I headed to the long, dark green microfiber couch I had considered a hidden treasure when I bought it so cheaply years ago from The Helping Hand Mission. Now it had someone's clothes hanging off of it (there was an equal chance of them being clean or dirty), a plate with a dark yellow crust stuck to it, a white stain (probably milk) spilling off the center cushion, and of course, plenty of crumbs sprinkled about like garnish on a dish at a fancy restaurant.

I moved the plate with the yellow crust over and brushed off some of the crumbs to make room for myself.

I dropped down, surrounded by the quiet. My thoughts began to bounce slowly off one thing to the next like the white ball in Pong, but I wished I didn't have to think at all. Never having been able to master the art of meditation, my mind would not be quieted without a colossal fight. The last dose of medication that the hospital had given me was slightly wearing, and at that moment, I wished I had more so I could just sleep. That's all I really wanted to do.

For so many years, I had fantasized about being able to slip peacefully into a coma for just a few months. All I wanted was to have a break. Right then felt like as perfect of a time as any for my coma fantasy to come true. I visualized myself curled into a tight ball, fetal-positioned, having been medically induced into a state of unconsciousness. With closed eyes, I was completely still and unaware of the world around me. What a grand vacation that would be!

Instead, I continued to sit on the couch with my head tilted back and my eyes closed. At that point, the kids weren't home and this, at least, was golden. I didn't know what I would do right then, or later that day, or that night, or the next day. There were no answers for me, at least none that my mind could have grabbed hold of right then. My senses adjusted to the foul smell, and I no longer noticed it. So, I sat in the dark, in the quiet, alone.

I don't know how long I had been sitting, but all the quiet made me conscious of my breathing. It was much too loud. I know I mentioned before that loud breathing bothers me immensely, and it bothers me even when it's my own. I tried taking measured breaths that aren't quite as deep. They must have become too shallow because I started getting light-headed. Sweat began to roll like tears from under my breasts and down to my stomach.

Trying to resume my normal breathing cadence was difficult at that point because I was paying too much attention to every breath and couldn't catch a natural rhythm. Pushing the clothes off the couch and onto the floor, I lay down on my side with my knees to my chest and my arms folded around both sides of my head. I was still wearing my blue, non-skid hospital socks. I really didn't know what to do.

If I were able to become addicted to drugs or alcohol, this kind of thing wouldn't be so difficult. It's my estimation that addicts are largely people with diagnosed or undiagnosed mental illness. The idea of being able to dose yourself into a state of numbness sounds divine. Erase the past, forget the present, who cares about the future...all available through a few gulps, inhalation, or a carefully placed needle. The problem is I'm just too damn lucid all the time.

The detrimentally repetitive thoughts that escalate clinical depression are hard to shake. Mentally talking yourself out of these lines of rumination seems impossible. It's like an annoying pop song that keeps playing on the radio. No matter how many times you try to change the channel, it blasts from every station. There are moments when you may get a commercial break or a decent song might play in between. These are the times when you try to fight through the thoughts and rustle up some hope to keep on going. But, eventually the same song comes back on, and you naturally start singing right along with it.

I wish I could disintegrate. Or just slowly melt through the couch then through the floor into another dimension. I try making up in my head where I'd go. But the place I would want to get to doesn't even exist in my fantasies. There's nowhere on earth or in imagination that appeals to me. I just want to be gone. And even now (at what I consider a reasonably sane point), the idea of death rationally doesn't seem that bad. Okay, you're dead. Your life is over. People miss you—some quite a lot. But in the grand scheme of things, one lifetime is an insignificant blip in the universe. Given the history of all things, one lifetime barely even registers. So, the allure of death is still present in my contemplation even without any major mental hiccups.

I believe in heaven and eternity, and I vaguely remember a Bible verse saying something along the lines of people who long for the kingdom of heaven being blessed. That's basically longing for this world or life to be over, right? That's what I want. I mean, this world and this life are all right. They have their good quality points: natural wonders, a plethora of varied places to visit, good times to be had, lessons to learn, people to help, and a purpose to figure out. But all in all, heaven and eternity is where it's really at, right? Like a lifetime is to a universe, so is good to the bad in life. It's that same tiny, microscopic, miniscule blip. That being said, death offers something much better, and so it's understandable that I think about it a lot.

The moments of calm in the midst of all this darkness are the moments I conjure up the pleasantness of hanging myself. Looking at a beautiful tree, sometimes I'd think, "What a lovely way to die." In these imaginings, I see myself calmly tying the noose around my neck and giving a graceful leap into the air, ending it all. Swaying back and forth with a cool breeze, my eyes are closed, my body hangs loosely, and I am at peace. It's like an enchanting piece of art, and it brings me relief to visualize it.

Though it may come across a bit contrary, these thoughts are better than the desperate anguish of devouring the grief that depression brings. Still, I know ultimately, they're no good either. I don't suffer under the allusion that there will still be a pleasant eternity awaiting me should I decide to take my life into my own hands, literally. I believe in hell as well as heaven, and I also believe what people of most religions are taught. Suicides don't get a happily ever after on the other side either. So, I try not to let my mind go to the point of longing for death enough to want to induce it prematurely. Sometimes I just long for fate to take its nastiest turn with me. No one has yet convinced me that this rational is faulty, so I'll continue to believe it until then.

Sometimes I think people will not accept how serious this pain is and how I must fight it tooth and nail not to succumb to the allocated solution. They just won't get it until I walk into the River Ouse or gas myself with my kitchen oven. I'd say, "See, I told you this was real...it could not be helped...I was dying from the inside out...it wasn't just for attention after all!" And they'd all say, "Aha! But alas! It was all true after all! We were so wrong!" But I'm still here, so most of them will continue to pay it no mind, and some will even dismiss it altogether.

Lying there with my arms still wrapped around my head, I slid my fingers across the bones sticking out the side of my face by my temples as I ground my jaw. What the hell was I going to do?

What I needed was to do something outside of myself, so I dug into the purse that had been flung on the floor near the couch. Victorious, my hand emerged with my fingers wrapped around my cell phone. Sliding it open, I pressed the letter "i." I pressed it, pressed it, pressed it, pressed it, and again till there was a row of i's lined up uniformly like tiny soldiers off to war. The problem was I wanted hundreds of these i's, but my phone wouldn't produce more of them just because I held down the button. I had to press, release, and press again. The effort was too great, and my thumb was tired after about twenty, so I gave up. I shut my phone with a snap and let it slide out of my hand and onto the floor.

The figurative clock was ticking, and I knew my kids would show up sooner rather than later. No one ever wanted to keep them, and whenever they did, it was always with a constant choir of "when are you coming to pick them back up?"

Why couldn't I have a proper breakdown like a celebrity? After it had been announced that I was hospitalized for "dehydration," I'd have my nanny to care for my children while I went to a retreat for a couple months, got pampered, went kayaking, and did a bit of yoga. I guess when you're poor, you can't even afford to go crazy the right way.

Staring at my phone that had landed safely on a small pile of clothes, I knew I was sure to receive calls from the concerned family members and the few friends who knew what had happened. These calls, however, would not be enough protection from what I knew my mind was capable of convincing me to do. A few halfhearted phone check-ins on my well-being were just part of their civic duty for being acquainted with a crazy person. But to me, the point of these calls was always all too clear. I was just another thing to be checked off their to-do list:

- ✓ Pay the electric bill
- ✓ Get an oil change
- ✓ Pick up dry cleaning
- Make sure she hasn't killed herself today

These conversations are always insincere, awkward, and as short as possible. The last thing they are is helpful. But I don't blame the people who try. At least they bother cause a lot of others don't. It's probably the exact thing I would do if I were on their side of the fence.

Hours passed by, and I was still in the same position, lying on my couch. I was used to lying around during these bouts. They say sleeping a lot is a sign of depression. I don't know that I really sleep any more than the average person, but I'm sure I lie around much more. Maybe if it were not for my kids keeping me awake, I might be able to sleep for the majority of the day. Sleeping, after all, is an effective way to not have to think.

I was just tired all the time, really. The sadness was pretty consistent, but what I was overwhelmed by at the forefront of my consciousness was an unquenchable tiredness. My mind and body longed to just rest.

Lying around is worse than sleeping, though. It accomplishes nothing. If you sleep, at least you get actual respite. Lying doesn't do anything but suspend you in a state of semi-functioning. It gives you an ample chance to think of all you should be doing, and at the same time, to count the seconds of all the time you're wasting.

My intent is never to spend my days doing nothing; I am just sometimes unable to make myself move is all. I suppose my depression lives somewhere between my chest and my stomach weighing my entire body down, forcing non-movement. Gravity is certainly in cahoots with this disease.

As I am lying on my bed or couch or wherever I happen to be on any given day, I try to will myself to get up, be productive. I give myself time limits; ten more minutes and you must get up. I try giving myself small assignments to accomplish: pick out the kids' clothes for school, clean the bathroom sink, take the trash to the dumpster. I will, will, will myself to get up. But this never works. The minutes become hours, the light becomes dark, and I still haven't moved.

My mom used to call this laziness, and maybe that's all it really is.

In my continued state of motionlessness on the couch, I allowed my eyes to open again and survey the room. It was overwhelming, to say the least. In the corner of the living room, I noticed my plastic elastic bracelet. It was sitting on top of some books that were off the bookshelf. Before I had tattoos on my right arm, I wore this idiotic-looking bracelet a lot. It had repeating slivers of pink, green, yellow, orange, pink, green, yellow, orange. I'd have never in a million, trillion years bought it or worn it for fashion purposes. But it was quite wide and quite cheap. Though it was ugly, what was on the skin found beneath was always uglier. It served its purpose.

People sometimes make fun of my tattoos. They did even more so when all that was inked across the inside of my wrist was the word "Breathe." Catching a glimpse, people would ask to examine it more closely, then came the inevitable, "What does that mean?" The especially clever folks always said, "So you need a reminder to breathe?" laughing at their own stupid joke.

Depending on my level of familiarity with the person (or my level of patience and/or annoyance), I either smirked back and joined them with a purposefully fake laugh to make them uncomfortable, or I'd say, with no laughter at all, "Yes, sometimes I do," leaving them to dry up their chuckles on their own.

As with most of my tattoos, I didn't get the word "Breathe" placed on my body haphazardly. I considered it for a significant amount of time before I let the needle ever touch my skin. The word and the placing of this word were both especially deliberate.

I needed something that would, at the same time, be both strong and beautiful enough to stop me from what my mind urged me to sometimes do. I needed something I wouldn't want to ruin and something that would also help to redirect my thoughts. It'd serve a triple purpose by covering up any stubborn scars that were still visible. I always knew it had to be a word. Words are so important to me. Words are power. But I needed just the right word to accomplish such a major feat.

As with any undertaking, I set directly to it by praying, researching, and looking about anywhere for signs. I don't recall exactly how I came to consider the word "breathe," but when I read the extended definitions, I knew I had found just what it was that I was looking for.

breathe [breeth]:

1. to inhale and exhale
2. to pause and rest before continuing
3. to feel free of restraint
4. to give rest from exertion
5. to make manifest
6. **To Live!**

This tattoo, which was the second I've ever gotten (the first being a ridiculous ladybug on my big toe), was placed in freehand script. It had to be on my right wrist because my right wrist was always the victim of my grief. I have never cut anywhere else. Always a knife or a razor in left hand carving away at my right wrist.

The first time I cut myself, I was twelve years old. I don't think I'd ever heard of "cutting" back then, and I wonder how I ever had the inclination to do something so gruesome. Then again, I obviously did not invent the practice, so there must be some innate thing on the inside of us (us with the warped minds, that is) that inherently calls us to do it.

There had been plenty of times before then when I wanted to hurt myself, and plenty of times when I actually did. Each of these instances always began with me feeling like an idiot and being furious with myself. I would hit my head with objects (I remember in particular a baseball I kept in my room), grinding these things as hard as possible into my skull, or I'd bang my head against the wall. During the latter, I was always fearful of making too much noise and causing my brother, mom, or dad to hear me, so I never did get too out of control. I would lock my door, hit my head repeatedly, and cry quietly.

But it was on New Year's Eve, 1994, soon to be a brand spanking new 1995 that I actually cut myself. I was alone in my room. I don't remember where the other members of my family were—if my parents were out, if my brother was at a friend's or in his room across the hall. But I could not have been entirely home alone because I remember the climate of secretiveness. I remember my closed door.

I spent that evening watching the countdown to the New Year via MTV. I must've premeditated the cutting because I already had a knife in my room, and I was waiting for a specific moment before I began. I planned on slicing myself for each second of the final ten-second countdown, and at the end of it, I'd have ten open wounds. As the timer closed in on the final moments and everyone from Times Square cheered me on, I began: ten...nine...eight... seven...six..., but I faltered, not realizing that I didn't quite have the speed to keep up with one cut per second. I'm sure I ended up with only about six or seven. The last couple came well after all the New Year's kissers had parted. My arm was sore and puffed up under each bloody line like the lips of the devil. I felt defeated in about a million ways, but I tried to get these final cuts onto my skin. It hurt too much to reach ten. Everything hurt too much, and I could barely see anything at all through the tears in my swollen eyes.

Since then, there have always been periods of time where not a day will go by that I don't think of cutting myself, driving off the road, or visualize myself hanging. Some (but a little surprisingly, not all) of my friends encourage me to go to the doctor during these slumps. I never want to go, though. There's a possibility (maybe a high probability) that I should be taking medication consistently to get my thoughts and mood under control. But for one, I don't want my mind to be hindered long-term. For all the wrong it does me, it does me a lot of right too. Maybe all those messed up chemical proportions make me think differently than most people and not just in the bad ways either. I don't want to lose that, not yet at least.

Besides, I've learned that, along with most people in life, you can't offer a doctor 100% full disclosure. If I strolled in to see a therapist or psychiatrist during these dark times and told them, "Hey, I think about injuring myself daily, and sometimes I talk to people who aren't really there," I'd be back in the hospital in a fraction of a second. Obviously, I just tried to be honest about the mildest expression of this illness, and they locked me up and threw away the key straightaway. I don't have the time for these hospitalizations. Like I said before, there are the kids to consider.

For two (or maybe I'm on three now; I lose count), I don't want them experimenting new cocktails of medicines on me to see what works. The side effects of these drugs are no freaking joke. They can range from just making you feel shitty physically (tired, dizzy, nauseous—all sensations that I despise) or they can flat-out kill you or make you want to kill yourself even more than you might already want to. I don't have anyone around me to monitor my progression with any new prescription drugs right now. The only people I see on any consistent basis are my children. They may have many responsibilities well beyond their years, but this is not one I'm willing to add to their load.

Since having gotten my blade blockade tattoo, I hate to admit it, but I have cut myself again. However, I am proud to say, it's not been often. The visual reminder has worked wonders in being the last defense in helping me fight this nasty compulsion. Years later and after adding several other tattoos around the first, my forearm is a now a collage of various images with differing levels of meaning. It remains the final barricade standing between me and myself.

***

70

Dry Bones

my pastor says
> *the greatest indicator of a child's success*
> *is the presence of their father*

I inspect the church's carpet, search
for all I might've been between the pieces of visible dirt
I memorize my children and grandchildren
wonder if I might turn down my plate
to ward off teenage pregnancies and incarceration
renounce wickedness to shield them this lethal absence
> I fear for my daughters
> I fear for my son
> > who no longer asks where his dad has gone
> pray for a grandson
> > who does not yet know all that he lacks

the past proves a history of generational curses
> his theory, sound
and my love too thin to cover the multitude of sins
from the men who have left blood on our thresholds
if little girls turned mothers are proof of this truth,
> it is complete
then where did Adam go
and what about the raising of dead things

71

Some things are better left unsaid. And there are some things I wish I didn't have to say at all. But I suppose it's hard to grasp the full context of a story when major parts have been omitted. Omission. What a loaded idea. Is it a lie to omit? I've always believed so, but here I am wishing to partake in such a sin. I swore to be as truthful as I could be, and it wouldn't be the truth unless I shared this.

But I will warn you now that we will walk together along a path, and at some point along our journey, we will come to the end of that path. And at the end of that path, there will be a door. This door will be shut, and it will be locked. We will both understand that I have the key to unlock this door. However, I will stand unwilling to open it. Behind this door are people—a father, fathers. And locked behind this door is where I intend for them to stay.

You'll understand that there's a pain that goes beyond mental illness, poverty, parenthood, beyond even death. The people who've administered this dose of pain do not belong in this story. Perhaps it's my form of punishment for the crimes I've convicted them of committing. Nevertheless, I have and will continue to avoid their mention as much as it is possible.

Of course, all progeny, including myself, are the products of men and women. You must know I have a father. You will assume my children also bear this same condition. That's as much as I will say about this matter for now.

With that out of the way, I'll tell you that I had my first child, a daughter, at the ripe age of sixteen. I lost my virginity and got myself pregnant. My high school science teacher told my class that it was virtually impossible to get pregnant the first time you have sex. She wasn't using me as an example or anything, and to be quite honest, I wasn't paying much attention to all the biological reasoning she offered. But I did interject that it wasn't true. It happened to me. When I think back to moments like that, I don't even recognize myself. The brazenness to defy a teacher, out loud, in front of an audience—all things I avoid at all costs now. Even if I know that I know something, most of the time I'd rather let someone spout off utter nonsense than to speak up and correct them. Not that I'm afraid (well perhaps in some instances), but mostly because I don't care enough.

I digress. I was sixteen and pregnant before MTV made that a thing. I was a sophomore in high school with a due date the fall quarter of my junior year. Ignorance is bliss because had I possessed the good sense to be as terrified as I should be, I wouldn't have survived. But there I was. Waking up at the crack of dawn for unbearably early classes, sprinting out of English to vomit up my mostly-digested pancake breakfast, carrying around a bottle of Pepto Bismol and swigging it down like a Coca-Cola.

A lot of my peers thought I was lying about my pregnancy. I didn't find this out until after the fact when one of them had the guts to admit to me they too thought I'd been faking. I can't imagine what anyone would get out of faking such a thing, but I guess even the most unfortunate situation has its payoff in one way or another.

This was 1998 and pre-everyone having a cellphone. This was when pagers were at their height and no longer just for doctors or drug dealers. You were cool if you had a pager in any color other than black and bonus points if it clipped on horizontally. I think I eventually convinced my parents that I was not in fact selling drugs and was able to get one myself. Mine was black and vertical, though.

My teachers during this period of my life stand out in sore contrast. There were two that showed me such kindness and such grace, I wish I had the opportunity to thank them after all this time. Mrs. Behun was an assistant teacher in my social studies course, and she radiated genuine compassion. She offered me a place to rest when my tender body and mind needed respite from the crowds. She encouraged me, and for some reason, she believed in me. I won't ever forget her.

Ms. Woodward was my sewing teacher. She was a much older woman from another time and a simpler pace, and she had every right to judge me and leave me on my own. But instead, she advised me not to eat the school's lunch because she didn't feel it was nutritious enough for my baby. She instructed me to buy a Cup of Noodles and welcomed me to heat it up and eat it in the privacy of her classroom. Cup of Noodles is just dried ramen in a styrofoam cup with some peas and carrots floating about, so being older and wiser, I now question the nourishment it provided, but without question, the sentiment was priceless.

Then of course, there were others. Others who weren't so kind. Those who rolled their eyes at me when I asked to use the restroom. The ones who made smart remarks at my expense without a moment's pause to consider the impact. And those who expected failure from me.

Again, I digress. I told you this time was pre-cell phone to explain how I broke the news to my mom. With my stomach full of knots, as well as a baby, I wrote her a letter one sleepless night before school. I couldn't tell you the exact contents of the letter, but it did tell her that I would call her during my lunch hour from the school payphone. I mustered all the strength a coward who couldn't break the news in person could muster and left the letter somewhere I knew she would find it.

What a day. I learned nothing, and I was sick to my stomach. This time it wasn't from the baby. It was from the agony that every passing minute brought as I awaited to hear the fate my mom was going to dish out. During my lunch break while my peers ate Domino's in the cafeteria or rushed out to the McDonald's up the street, I made my way to the school's courtyard full of trailers to accommodate a growing number of students as well as a singular payphone. I'm sure by then a phone call cost .35. The increase from .25 always made me angry. A quarter made sense. Most people carried quarters. But a quarter and a dime felt unreasonable. After depositing the two coins, the only words I can remember from that conversation were, "I'm sorry," said often and through tears.

I had been indoctrinated since early childhood with the pro-life agenda, one that spans my family for generations, that abortion was never even a passing thought. My grandmother, aunts, and cousins all marched annually at the Right to Life rally in DC. Every single persuasive essay assigned to me from elementary, middle, and high school argued the virtues of pro-life and admonished the immorality of abortion. This was never an option.

Reflecting back, as I so often do, it turns out that no matter how old I get, I will forever be too young to have a child her age. So, while I'm sure most will agree that I was too young a girl to have that big baby at sixteen, turns out, I was also too young to have a five-year-old at twenty-one. Again, when I was thirty, I still wasn't quite old enough to be able to have a middle schooler. And I'll assume at sixty, someone will scrunch their face and turn their mouth sideways once they do the math against my age and determine I'm too young to have a forty-four-year-old child.

While I informed my mother of the news fairly early on, I had zero plans to tell my father. Without going into details, I'll just say I was no fan of his, and he was no fan of mine. We lived in the same house, so you'd think I must've gone to great lengths to hide my pregnancy. Except when someone only acknowledges your existence to bark an order to you, it's surprisingly simple. I put forth next to no efforts to conceal my expanding appetite, constant sickness, or growing stomach. I'd come home after school, heat up some ramen noodles in the microwave, and plop in front of the TV. He'd come in shortly afterward, order me to do the dishes or some other chore and retreat to the La-Z-Boy and Canadian Mist in his room.

This routine was going pretty well until I was eight months pregnant. My brother decided it was ridiculous for our father not to know, and he took it upon himself to inform *Him*. Even though it wasn't exactly his business, I don't harbor any ill feelings toward my brother for this action. I guess I get it.

His reaction was to be expected. Absolute dramatics along with all the woe-is-mes *he* could muster.

One positive outcome of telling my mom I was pregnant was that she insisted I graduate high school early. This meant me taking a co-op class that gave me an additional credit I'd need to graduate as well as me taking

English 12 at night school.

Well, my English 11 teacher was sure to let me know that no student had ever been successful in taking both English 11 and 12 at the same time. Again, that youthful naivety left me unswayed. I went to a separate school at night that was generally filled with troubled teens who were either failing or had been kicked out of their traditional schools. I was neither, but I was a teen mom. So, I belonged there just the same.

When it was all said and done, I successfully completed the English 11 work I was expected to do while I was out for six weeks on maternity leave. In fact, I was so successful at this task that the same English teacher asked if she could keep my papers as examples for other students in the future. Being the benevolent individual I am, I obliged.

Needless to say, I came back from maternity leave, aced my French exam, passed my English 12 with flying colors, and graduated high school a year ahead of schedule. Having skipped my entire senior year, I wasn't exactly prepared for college. I had only taken a practice SAT at the beginning of my junior year (that I didn't study for), but that score was going to have to be good enough to get me in somewhere.

I applied for three local schools and got accepted into two. I chose an HBCU over an all-girls school and trudged my way (with my new daughter) to a degree. I ended up using the extra year I had from high school to get my Bachelor's. Having a semester struggling without daycare really set me back.

College is where I met the next *Him*. It was also where and when I had my son. My pregnancy with him was stressful and complicated. Very early on, so early in fact I didn't know I was pregnant, I had a pap smear that reported precancerous cells on my cervix. This result required a cervical biopsy.

It was an outpatient procedure during which I was to remain awake. I was cautioned to take some pain medicine before I went in, which I did, but I might as well have swallowed a couple of tic tacs for all the good it did me.

The doctor performing the biopsy had me hoisted up on the exam table typical of the ones in gynecologist offices. It had the stirrups for my feet, and I was instructed to slide down to the end of the table. I tried to relax and remembered not to hold my breath. Even now, I am taking deep and measured breaths to recall the incident in my own mind.

After inserting the metal thing that keeps you open while doctors mess about your cervix, she pulled out her first snipping tool, and she attempted to cut off a sample. I wish the word "attempted" carried more weight. It needs more weight in this instance. It needs all the weight in the world because try as she might, she removed nothing.

She brought out more tools, each as unsuccessful as the last. She poked, pulled, and cut on me while I tried my utmost to remain conscious. During her fight with my cervix, she did check on me a few times. But despite my pain and obvious torment, she continued undeterred in her quest to extract the cells.

At some point, she finally got what she needed, and it was over. However, I stayed on the table for at least an hour until I regained the strength to stand. In the meantime, nurses offered me crackers, juice, and fanned me to help in my struggle not to faint.

I found out that I was pregnant very soon after this procedure, and it meant that I had been pregnant when the doctor yanked and hacked my cervix. Ever since that biopsy up until he was born, I had sporadic and uncontrolled bleeding throughout my pregnancy.

Eventually, my obstetricians could not stop my bleeding, so I was put on bedrest about five months in. As much as I tried to follow orders and stay horizontal, I did have a five-year-old whom I needed to take care of. I wasn't the best patient, and I wish I was able to stay off my feet more than I did.

Along with the bleeding came the contractions. They weren't so bad at first, but they progressed to the point that I had to make several visits to the hospital. In most instances, they were able to give me some kind of medication that stopped the contractions and sent me back home.

One particularly stressful day, *He* made me upset to the point of crying. I cried to the point of hyperventilation. And I hyperventilated to the point of contracting. Per my new routine, I proceeded to the hospital, but this time, they couldn't get the contractions to stop. I needed to go to UNC, a larger and more specialized hospital. So, in the ambulance I was packed to take the forty-minute ride to Chapel Hill. I was only twenty-seven weeks pregnant.

This was my first time in an ambulance, and I hope it will be my last because it pissed me off. The contractions hurt like a mother, and that ambulance must've worn its shocks all the way down because every pebble on the road bounced me around like I was on safari. The EMT folks had casual conversations while I was sure I was dying. And although most of the trip involved highway driving, they drove at what felt like a glacial pace.

About three years later, we arrived at the hospital, and I remember next to nothing until I got to a room. Doctors, nurses, and other medical staff surrounded me and started pumping me full of medications. One told me I was going to be injected with steroids to accelerate the baby's lung development, and while they did that, they were going to get some other meds in me to once again try to stop the contractions.

Whatever they did worked because the next thing I knew, it was morning time, and I was waking up in my own hospital room. I had slept through the night, and my contractions had stopped.

It was March, and my son wasn't due until June. I started to worry, thinking of spending the next several months stuck in the hospital while they doped me up to keep the baby inside. I was anxious about my daughter and how she would be taken care of. I had several visitors, and a few days later, I celebrated my twenty-second birthday in a hospital bed.

Little did I know, my worries about spending months in the hospital would prove to be unnecessary. Just about a week after I was admitted, I began to develop a fever. When the doctor examined me, he told me they were concerned that it may be indicative of the baby having an infection. They needed to induce labor.

After moving me to a labor and delivery room, they gave me both an epidural and the labor-inducing drug. Unlike with my daughter, this epidural worked like a dream. It worked so well that, in fact, I went to sleep during most of my labor. I had to be unceremoniously woken up when it was time

78

to push, and I tried to convince everyone to let me sleep a little longer, but they weren't having it.

Begrudgingly, I got up and assumed the position. Two pushes later, out he came. The tiniest person I had ever seen. He was wet and covered in the fetal hair that usually falls off in utero between thirty-two to thirty-six weeks gestation. At only twenty-eight weeks, he didn't make it that far. In other words, my son was twelve weeks, or three months, early. He was two pounds, fourteen ounces, and I thought he looked like a cute, little hairy rat.

My precious boy was alive and breathing, and I was exhausted. After spending a few minutes with him, he was taken away to the NICU where his tiny, fragile body would get the assistance it needed to survive.

I remained at the hospital for about another week and was wheeled down to see my baby at least once a day. The room was lined with small plastic boxes with two holes for hands. For the first day or so, he couldn't come out of his box. He had what looked like a minuscule version of sunglasses covering his eyes, and he was under a light to prevent jaundice. He also had a tube in his nose and an IV in his hand. The diaper that was about an inch and a half across looked too large for him. The sight of him, along with the hormones running riot through my body, made me emotional. I whimpered and cried each time I visited him.

Eventually, he was stable enough for me to hold him, and I did. His long, frail body felt like I was holding only a bundle of small blankets. The skin that covered his tiny bones was wrinkled and thin. He never opened his eyes.

Being discharged was one of the hardest things I've had to do. Leaving your child in the hospital will never be easy for any mother. He had to stay until he was able to perform three biological functions on his own—eat, breathe, and regulate his body temperature.

He stayed in Chapel Hill for three weeks, and I took that trip many times to keep him company. After that time, he was deemed stable enough to be transferred to a closer hospital. This was most welcomed news as it enabled me to see him daily.

After a total of six weeks, I was allowed to bring him home. I believe he got up to about six pounds, but the preemie outfit I bought for him was still baggy. His car seat threatened to swallow him up, even with all the extra cushions to hold him upright.

My youth and ignorance served me yet again in this circumstance. I had no idea just how bad it could've been for him to be born that premature. If I were in that situation now, I'd be terrified. I don't think I understood the gravity of it all. He could've been severely disabled. He could've died. But instead, he was a miracle.

Between a lack of daycare and giving birth, my college years were slightly extended. However, I still managed to graduate. I walked across the stage with my six-year-old daughter and brand new one-year-old son in the audience. I also walked across the stage four months pregnant.

The tales of my third pregnancy are no less drama-filled than the first two. Perhaps it was even more so. When it was all said and done, I gained only fifteen pounds (six of which was my baby). I blame the stress.

I was raising my two children alone, finishing up undergrad, all while growing a human inside of me. Times were hard. I'll spare the details of these grueling nine months and skip right to her birth.

My grand finale also came early. Not nearly as early as her big brother, but she was three weeks early and would be considered premature by the doctors. She was the only pregnancy during which I experienced my water breaking naturally. The feeling was foreign, and at first, I doubted what I felt. It didn't take me long to realize this was the real thing.

My contractions weren't yet unbearable, so I got my kids settled and was able to make my way to the hospital. Her birth was straightforward. A fair amount of contractions that lasted for a few hours, some pain meds, an epidural, a bit of pushing, and *voila*. Little baby girl.

Now here's where the story gets good (or being on the receiving end, gets awful). Seeing as how my daughter entered the world a little earlier than expected, I wasn't quite prepared for her. The house wasn't as tidy as I'd have liked, and her essentials weren't yet in place. So, once I was in my recovery room and the baby was doing okay, I sent *Him* and my son home to get things in order. My oldest was with my friends, so I'd get to rest for a bit.

This was 2005 when cellphones were everywhere but did not have nearly the capabilities as they do today. Phone numbers and contact information were not yet stored in cellphones, and as I lay there, I realized I needed to call my sisters to let them know the baby had arrived.

I called *Him* to ask that he look in my phone book to give me the numbers. The phone rang and rang in my ear until the line picked up. An unfamiliar male voice told me that he was not available and hung up. Angry and assuming this was one of his ill-mannered friends, I called right back. The voice answered again, but this time they provided more information.

"He has done something really bad, and he's in a lot of trouble." The next voice I heard was *Him*, "I'm sorry." And the line went dead.

As one might imagine, this ambiguous dialogue left me a bit hysterical. I could not begin to make up in my head what was going on. Where was my car that he had been driving? How would I get home? Most importantly, where in the world was my *son*?

These questions would be answered when my cell rang a few minutes later. The mysterious voice on the other end was identified as a police officer. *He* had attempted to sell drugs at a gas station to an undercover cop. With my son.

The levels of hysteria were rising, and I felt trapped and helpless in my hospital bed. I made several tearful phone calls. My mom was going to the gas station to pick up my car (thank God it wasn't towed or impounded). The friend who had my oldest daughter was on the way back to the hospital. And the police officer was bringing my son.

I still think to this day how different this story could've been had he made a less compassionate choice. But there I was, fresh from having given birth and now also taking care of my seventeen-month-old son in a hospital room. After a while, my friend took my two older children home with her, and I was left alone.

He would later call me from jail, begging to use my credit card to bail him out. I refused but was generous enough to call his sister on three-way to coordinate with his parents. If they wanted to spend their money this way, I figured it was their choice because I knew with the utmost certainty that I would not.

By this time, the hospital staff had gotten wind of what happened. A social worker visited me, and the nurses made the executive decision to take the baby to the nursery for the night. I was grateful and needed to sleep.

As it tends to do, life happened in and out and up and down during the years in between my children's births and my next hospitalization. Good decisions and bad ones, happiness, sadness, and stories that you might feel were hyperbole or pure fabrication could be shared. But those we will save for another day. For now, I'll choose the sleep of that blessed and dreadful day in the maternity ward and wake up three years later.

***

Be / Long • ing

i

If you asked my name, I'd begin by telling you
the one I was born with, learned to write by its letters

before I realized they could be laid down as weapons
knew it as I know myself, then as easy as an exhale

to blow dry a dab of whiteout (or as quick
as an execution by guillotine)

replaced it for a man who came along
offering me his name three times

        once for the Father
        the Son
        and again, for the Holy Ghost

He promised to build a palace from our intentions
so I adorned the divinity of that second name

We gave it (recompense) to the seeds still covered in dirt
        and now that he's gone

I hoard some rightful indignation in his stead
refuse the former, because my father

        (who still pokes fingers in clay)
was never mine

He belongs to the same league of men
who donate names freely

without the blood-loss of covenant
who drop them off like a pair of shoes every other school year

instead of the daily shackles they are

83

So now this second name rolls off my lips

like an obligation or an obstacle, rolls off
like a dead thing does

                i

If you asked me about this name here
I'll tell you of self-creation, and share the story of how

a 'K' was conjured for Joanne
so little boys would read about Harry

And because I want men
            (all men)

to hear my voice
            to tremble

I stole from my grandfather
the name he never knew was his

the name I found disintegrating
in his trailer home, tucked between

the Holy Bible and the black and white photo
of my father (and the woman he left in Vietnam)

I mask myself in my grandfather's masculinity, fool them
make myself

            less
poisonous

so not even their subconscious
can reject this loathsome, wondrous femininity

This name, self-given, can't be confiscated (a payment
for death before death), yet does not belong to me still

i

If you asked where I am from
I'll rattle off cities and states

which you'd have been to or never heard of
Give you years or ages

say
    yes
my father was in the military

but that was before I was born
    (Vietnam. yes, yes)

So
    no
that's not why we moved so much

It was his job or indiscretions
that landed us one place or the next

I'd tell you I don't remember much, except a yellow home in Kentucky
wood chips and a rose-colored childhood left in Michigan

a three-month old's memory of nothing from the place I was born
lawlessness in the military town

my first taste of salt in sandwiches and white supremacy
at the beach, and finally, here

by default, here (where I spend the time I own
    inside my head)

So this is the home I'll give you
if that is what you're after

I'll garnish my answers, ask what you're in the mood to eat
feed you simplicity or a detail of intrigue

Once you swallow it down, wipe the corners of your mouth
     say goodbye

I'll cover my eyes, split open my head
go on asking

       where is my name
       and when is home

I don't remember my kids coming back the evening of my second release from the psychiatric hospital. I'm sure there wasn't any ceremony to it. Whoever dropped them off probably did me the favor of feeding them, and that was good because I would have made them eat whatever they could find.

They were probably happy to see me, and I was probably happy to see them, but in a different sort of way. Most of the time I could only feel sorry for them. Some people view those who are suicidal as being full of self-pity, but I believe it's not that at all really.

You don't sit around going "Woe is me. Why do I always get the short end of the stick?" You just kinda sit around most of the time thinking you're shit. Not even worthy of the short or long end of anything. You don't rationalize and bemoan how life isn't fair to you. You are just useless and hopeless and pretty much hate that the people you love have to have anything to do with you. It's self-hate not self-pity, and when you're in it, you believe there's no way out, and that's when your mind can no longer be trusted.

A lot of times you don't tell anyone when you get really down or suicidal. Contrary to popular opinion, you don't not tell people out of selfishness either. It's quite the opposite. You are such complete and utter crap that taking yourself out would be an act of benevolent charity. Like some form of community service. So convinced of your worthlessness and the burden of your sadness that you believe it's the best thing for everyone: your parents, your best friends, your boyfriend or girlfriend if you've got one, even your children if you have those. That's the most unfortunate part. You're so below low that you actually believe nonsense like that.

But I did pity my kids. I was sorry that they had to have an unbalanced person for a mother. I was sorry that I was their only parent. That guilt probably made me more unbalanced because I just hated myself all the more for what I was to them. A person who didn't do well picking out their fathers, and they suffered for that on top of everything else. I was sorry that their lives had to be less than they deserved because of who I am.

I just don't know if it can be helped. I think my mind is permanently warped. People talk of chemical imbalances and things like that. I've paid particular attention to that term from a young age. I sensed, without really knowing, that what was wrong in my mind was exactly what they were talking about. I have this visualization of the Lady Justice holding her balanced scale. Except this scale is sitting smack in between the right and left lobes of my brain. On each plate of the scales sits a tiny pyramid comprised of a white, crystalized chemical substance. I know they should have equal amounts of the chemicals in precisely the right proportions weighing exactly the same, and they ought to be floating parallel to one another. But mine has a little too much of this and a little too little of that, causing one plate to be as high as it can go while the other is touching the floor of my brain.

A mind or a psyche or a soul can only take so much. If a brain is filled with too much sadness or a disproportionate amount of any negative emotion for an excessive period of time, it is bound to have dire and probably long-lasting consequences. By my reasoning, it's inevitable.

The truth of my current situation was that I had had a mental breakdown, and I was scared it would happen again. This fear crept up like an incoming tide, but when it hit, it was with the full force of a tsunami. It at once overwhelmed and consumed me and became the foundation for every choice I made. I was afraid to leave my home.

After I left the hospital for the second time, I ended up making my apartment my own padded cell. Frightened of every place, person, sound, and thought that could tip the scale for me and send me off the deep end, I blocked myself off as much as I could from all possible sensors. I'd sit on my couch, stark still, scared to move for days on end. My phone would go off; I'd watch my employer's number pop on, and I would just stare at it, ringing until silence. Listening to messages from concerned friends. Still not moving. I feared the words that I might hear if I answered. I couldn't take that chance anymore. I was too fragile.

I was afraid to be by myself, but I was also too embarrassed for company. Sometimes I'd force myself to do the dishes, so my children wouldn't have to debate eating dinner with crackers as their utensils or trying to wash one of the decrepit forks in the overflowing sink.

Besides, I had nothing to say to anyone other than myself anyway. I was just scared. So scared. Fearful that at any moment, I might break. I was frail. Anything could happen that would set this chain of events back into motion. Next time, I might break and never be put back together again. Fear became my consistent condition. I could not go to work. It was completely out of the question. I wished I never had to go again.

As crazy (or crazier) as it seems, I found a bit of solace in tabloids. Seeing people whose lives I had once envied going through such hardships and misery somehow comforted me. These celebrities' greatest tragedies and greatest sadnesses (real or invented by some creative journalist) got blasted everywhere for all the world to see. What shame; what humiliation!

I don't say this to be cruel. For all my flaws, I am much too empathetic a person to rejoice in the suffering of others. But the comfort I found was in the comparison I could make. If my life's shame known only to myself is so unbearable at times, how do these individuals ever smile again? How do they manage to go on? If they did not die instantly on the spot from the shame, then surely there is hope for me as well.

People's mental issues aren't reported with any believable truths attached, so I don't pay these types of stories much regard. The thing I find most consoling are the cases of celebrities who are/were married, have children, and have been suspected of being cheated on. Anyone over the age of fifteen knows this betrayal always seems like the worst pain when you're in the moment, but I believe overcoming it is one of the greatest life experiences one can ever have. Once you learn that this mountain of pain can be healed, it gives you the greatest hope in all future heartaches to come.

And so, this was my way of life for the next couple of months:

agoraphobia, tabloids, scraping by. I rode the high tide of fear, and with no traumatic aftermath to feed it, it began to ebb. With the fear subsiding, I began to function again. Not completely, but I could go to work (though I missed more days than I was present). I could be expected to keep a reasonable amount of food in the house while also keeping the lights on. I wouldn't describe it as thriving, but I wanted to be alive versus being dead, and that could be counted as a vast improvement.

My days were seemingly one in the same. This repeating sameness is how I recall many years of my life. I would go to work or not. Pay bills or worry about how to pay them. Figure out how and what to feed myself and my children. Do all the things you had to do when you have kids: change diapers, take them to school, wash them, etc. I'd watch TV, read a book, think of how to rise above this cycle of nothingness, find no viable answers, and go to sleep.

Life smoothed itself out and continued its placid, mediocre course for almost two months—right up until the day my mom called me and told me my sister had cancer.

**

part 2

I fold myself
in half

nose to knees
and once more
offer you all
my space
         collapse
inward
the light
a haloed glow
mere flicker
dark upon dark
         disappear
pluck out each hair
strand by strand
offer myself to be
         devoured
tighten my smile
unhinge my jaw
turn inside out
swallow
whole

I needed to grab ahold of something. The small bathroom that I had escaped into at Starbucks suddenly started moving all around me. It was like when you're at a stoplight waiting for the signal to change and the car next to you with a manual transmission starts rolling backward. You press on your brakes a little harder to make sure you're not the one who's moving and about to collide with the car ahead of you. At that moment, I couldn't tell if it was me or the rest of the world that was spinning.

My voice was shaky, though I tried to control it. I just knew my mom would think I was being overly dramatic just because, and I didn't want her to think that. After all, she was being calm and cool. No nonsense, just the facts. There was no alarm in her voice. No reason for fear. But Lord knows I was panicked and terrified nonetheless. The same fear that I'd managed to abate and keep at a safe distance for the past couple of months flooded over me, and once again, I was drowning in it.

I had to remember I was in public and with my children. It was Christmas time, and we were at the shopping center just a couple miles from our house. They always had free holiday events for kids, and we had been coming faithfully for the past couple of years.

There was a station to make cheap Christmas ornaments out of foam cutouts and stickers. The kind that usually won't make it past Christmas present. Santa was always there, and they'd give you free Polaroid pictures of your children sitting on his lap. But the best part was the horse and carriage rides through the parking lot. It was too short and the setting was all wrong, but a horse and carriage is always fun no matter what. That year would be the last time I would ever take my kids to that shopping center to ride the horse and carriage.

"Paula has cancer."

I had heard the word "cancer" used against my family once before. My mom had been diagnosed with breast cancer four years before, and she ended up being okay. But this word sitting inside this particular phrase coming through the phone in my mother's voice carried a different heft.

"Paula has cancer."

A prize-winning fighter's right hook squarely made contact with my unblocked chest, and the wind was knocked clean out of me. Once my mother had concluded relaying all the information that was known at present and the call ended, I broke. Sliding down the wall, I sat on the cold, hard, germ-ridden floor and sobbed. This crying spell would be the first of many endless bouts over the next few months, carrying on through the next few years. It wasn't the same as the ambiguous crying of depression. These tears had a specific phrase attached to each drib.

"Paula has cancer."

⁕

What I knew was this: Paula had been having back pains for a while, thought to have possibly been a hernia, and she had been going to see a pain specialist. One night, the pain must've become unbearable because she was taken to the emergency room. Assuming she had fluid in her abdomen, the doctors went to drain it, and when they opened her up, they found it. "It" being cancer. I believe someone used the phrase, "the cancer was everywhere." Being painfully naïve at the time, I didn't realize how bad that statement, in and of itself, was.

Maybe it was lucky Paula never made it as scheduled to visit our sister Charity, who was temporarily living in England with her family at the time. Though maybe it was not lucky. Maybe she would have been better off avoiding everything that came next. After the cancer was discovered, it was decided that she would need to have surgery. They removed her appendix, as they suspected the cancer may have originated from there. As it so happened, it had not. They were eventually able to determine that she had a Krukenberg tumor (if you decide to look up the phrase, "Kruckenberg," I guarantee you will not find the information given pleasant in any way), and so her uterus and ovaries were also removed.

The metastasized cancer was so widespread, the doctors could not establish its true origin until about a month later. It wound up being stomach cancer—aggressive, Stage 4, low survival rate. By the time of this determination, it was too far gone and inoperable.

When I went to visit her that Christmas, she looked okay, just a little slow from the recovery of the initial surgeries. She hadn't started chemotherapy yet, so she was still mostly herself. Our sister Angee had flown in from California for the holiday. This was a rare treat, as we (each individual member of our family) often go many years without seeing her. She is the only one of us on the West Coast. Due mostly to financial straits, we find it difficult to make it across the country regularly.

We had moments as we've always had. Lots of time spent in the kitchen figuring out how to keep our small army of children fed. Time sitting around watching TV shows and time preparing for the big day, Christmas.

Paula and Ray became nearly fanatical in their quest for getting their three children laptops and other big-ticket items for Christmas. I was not alone in echoing the sentiment that this was an extravagance ludicrous for a twelve, ten, and eight-year-old. Our initial reaction to these elaborate presents was probably a form of denial. What were they thinking wasting all that money on something the kids probably wouldn't take proper care of, much less appreciate, at their ages? When in reality, Paula feared the worst and wanted to make this Christmas as memorable as possible for her babies. Just in case.

∗∗∗

Taking my kids to church on Wednesday nights has been a part of our routine for almost as long as I remember. We may have missed a service here and there, but for the most part, that's where you could find us if you happened to be looking for us midweek. Sometimes it was nice just to get a break from the kids as they went to their classrooms (this was one of the only breaks I had from them when school was over), sometimes I needed spiritual nourishment to hang onto what hope remained in me, and sometimes we'd turn up purely for the physical nourishment in the form of the free homecooked meal they provided.

The Wednesday after hearing my sister's diagnosis was tough, to say the least. Every day after that was tough, but somehow I rallied my troops, and we made it to church. After eating the generous portion of spaghetti with a side salad and dinner roll, it was time for us to part and go to our respective destinations.

Having gotten my kids to their classrooms, I should have been walking over to join the adults in the main sanctuary. But this time I couldn't. The smile I had been faking the past hour had expired. I couldn't get the corners of my lips to curl up or my teeth to show themselves anymore. My eyes began to water, and I knew I needed to hide.

Moving as quickly as possible through the parking lot, I got into my car and closed the door fast behind me. No longer able to hold back anymore, a wail from deep within my gut burst forth. And another after that. And another. There was nothing inside of me left that could hide the sorrow that was born with each thought of my sister, which now whirled unceasingly through my mind.

Enveloped in my own grief, I did not notice anyone was still outside, and the slight tapping on my window might as well have been a shotgun's blast. The instant fright shut down my wailing but only long enough to notice the woman standing next to my car door.

Nearly doubled over with my head on the steering wheel, low moans still escaping my parted lips, I hit the button on the door panel and rolled down my window.

She didn't bother to introduce herself, and I was glad for it. She started talking, and the words she said calmed me enough that I was able to tell her what troubled me.

"My sister has cancer."

She didn't judge me. Outwardly, at least. She was compassionate enough that I wasn't embarrassed. I felt understood. As if my anguish was justified.

After she left me, my breath evened, and I sat in the quiet. I was not well enough to go into service. I feared my eyes would have betrayed me even if I had tried, so I remained in my car until everything was over. I picked up my kids, and we went back home.

During this period, I found myself carrying two pictures of Paula in a blue spiral bound student calendar. Although I've long since been a student, I am still best able to function with my year broken down from August to August.

One of the photos I brought with me was a picture taken outside of my mother's home. Paula's walking through the archway that leads to our mom's front door. Her blonde hair is mane-like, but you can tell, even with the distance, that she has it professionally highlighted. Wearing jeans and a fitted, forest green three-quarter length sleeved shirt, she looks effortlessly put together.

I can't tell from her expression if she knows the picture is being taken. Her eyes aren't focused on the camera, but rather cast slightly down toward her daughter who's walking directly in front of her.

Her daughter, Maggie, isn't looking at the camera either. Her broad smile is aimed at something left of the camera's lens and shows off dimples so deep they cause strangers to stop and fawn over her. Paula is bent slightly and is reaching to hold her daughter's outstretched hands. It looks like her little girl could be walking with her feet on top of Paula's because they're so close, but the picture is cut off and leaves you wondering. They're coming just under the archway, and looking at it now, she looks like an angel.

The second was taken inside our mom's house, and Paula is holding my son. Jack is just a baby, and she has her arms wrapped around him, pressing her cheek against his. The love she has for him emanates from the photo. Her child and mine. She loved all our kids so much. That's one of the things I admire most about her. There was never any doubt how much she loved them all.

Without invitation, I pulled out my calendar and produced these pictures, showing them to my therapist. Her reaction made me regret having done this.

"Why did you want me to see her pictures?"

I was at one of my becoming infrequent, but still regularly scheduled, therapy sessions after my departure from the nut house. I didn't need long to search for an answer to her question. I knew why I showed them. I knew why I carried them with me.

"Because I wanted you to see how young and beautiful she is."

In actuality, I needed to remind myself how young and beautiful she was. People her age with so much life and spirit left did not die from cancer.

She agreed that, yes, she was young and, yes, she was beautiful.

I guess even therapists have their limits because she stopped digging further into my statement the way she normally would have.

Even though she didn't ask, my response made me linger on why the hell I wanted to show everyone how youthful and pretty my sister was. Upon reflection, I think, in addition to comforting myself, I also wanted to prove to anyone who was willing to look that she didn't deserve to have stomach cancer. She appeared the epitome of health externally. She was much too young. She was beautiful in an enviable kind of way. You could tell by her pictures that she enjoyed her life. She was happy by choice and not by chance. I wanted everyone to see that this was unfair, and that it was complete bullshit.

My sister was everything I'm not. She's a blue-eyed, blonde-haired, All-American beauty. I'm not sure if my eyes are hazel, green, or a little bit of both. And I've just finally come to terms with my huge, curly, unruly hair.

Her All-American variety of beautiful contrasted starkly with my own, oft-described "exotic," beauty. Oh, how I detest that phrase. Everyone's been asking me the same question for as long as I can remember, "What are you?"

Paula was bubbly and personable, the variety that never met a stranger. I could quite possibly be the poster child for the antithesis of "bubbly" and "personable."

She was confident and happy. My bouts at the mental hospital should attest to the fact that I am neither. I was in awe of her. Being around my sister made me want to be a better person. A better homemaker, a better mother, the best me. She was sometimes blunt and honest in a way that could hurt your feelings. But instead of becoming defensive or rebelling against them, I just wanted to change.

Then other times she was so sensitive and thoughtful, you'd think she cherry-picked each word she gave you to avoid any conceivable offense. In the depths of one of the great calamities of my life, she sent me a greeting card. I don't think anyone else thought much to even pick up the phone to see if I was still hanging on. But here was this card. Outside of any holiday or special event. The outside was bright with colorful flowers spanning the rainbow. The inside had no Hallmark words, just her own handwritten note. She told me that a nice, happy life was possible, but I must take great care to make good decisions. It seems so simple, perhaps obvious. But this wisdom is something I wish someone would have told me just as plainly a lot earlier in life. I've thought of her words often and have passed on this advice to each of my children. I pray they understand their genuine importance.

✳✳✳

permanent dwelling

salivating with regret
memories collect on the tip of my tongue
slide back down my throat
choke the air that would have vibrated
into something beautiful,
like a song
or at least something useful,
like your name

this dried leaf caught in a wind chime
whose crude crackle of disintegration
is drowned out by metallic clanging
meant to elicit images of heavenly hosts
the translucent flutter of fairy wings
nothing whatsoever to do
with a gradual dying

without a tangible hand or hope to hold
on to, I remain no more
than some whirligig caught
in a tempestuous tornado of regret

no more than the loud hollow click
of a tight key turning the lock
to an empty house

Being worried and having anxiety is not the same thing. Being anxious and having anxiety is also not the same thing.

Innumerable times in my life I have been concerned over some future thing that could or would happen. I might have been nervous to the point of sleeplessness over something like having to make a presentation in front of a class. My stomach could have been filled with a lofty sickness at the thought of getting in trouble for some wrong I had committed. I might've been filled with absolute dread over the thought of some perceived heinous misfortune: infidelity, financial crisis even. But still none of these things are the type of anxiety that accompanies an anxiety disorder.

By the time my sister became ill, I had an intimate and knowing relationship with depression. We were so close that sometimes it might be difficult to tell where the depression ended and I began. Anxiety, however, was an unfamiliar arena. I, of course, had heard the term, but a passing superficial understanding was about as deep as my knowledge ran.

Soon enough, I'd learn that if depression was an inescapable dark cloud, anxiety was the violent cyclone of a fierce tornado.

My therapist described anxiety and depression as kissing cousins, and where you find one, you'll often find the other. If I had to rank which was worse, I'd give it up to anxiety. Depression is awful, I know, and it can kill you. Anxiety, though, is such a dreadful physiological and psychological combination that it can put an end to your life while you are, in fact, still living.

The uncontrolled irrational fear that causes your head to spin, your heart to beat out of control, and your sweat to pour is nothing short of paralyzing. Maybe the worst physical feeling I have ever experienced is the initial sensation of a panic attack rising. Not because it's physically unbearable, but because just knowing what is coming shuts down everything inside of me. The sick, almost indescribable tingle bubbling from within and the fire burning in my chest quickly covers my entire body from head to toe and means I will soon be trapped. Trapped inside my body and trapped inside my head. It means I will be afraid to be alone and afraid to be around other people. I'll be afraid to go to bed and afraid to get out of bed. The cyclone of fear picks up momentum as it sweeps up one fearful thought after another.

I've learned that sometimes I am able to talk myself down from a panic attack. The moment I detect that tingle inside of me, I start to fight. I try to control my breathing and slow my heart rate. I try to capture every thought and hold it hostage so that it doesn't end up the other way around, holding me hostage. Sometimes I am successful, and sometimes I am not.

I've also learned two other things: the more powerfully I allow that prickle to become a whirlwind inside of me and the more frequent it comes, the more apt this condition is to spiral out of control with panic attacks coming more and more often. Conversely, the longer I can manage to keep these attacks at bay, the less often they will arise and the longer I will go between incidents.

Just as I can pinpoint the time where depression started its takedown of my mind, I can also pinpoint when anxiety took its turn. When my sister became ill, I concurrently became afflicted with a panic disorder.

Over the years, I've become aware of my own personal triggers, and this helps in keeping my head straight. I know that if I ever become ungodly tired from a lack of sleep, I will have a panic attack. If I ever drink alcohol to the point where I am not in complete control of my body but my thoughts remain clear (those damn thoughts), I will have a panic attack. If I ever have a foreign pain that I can mentally attribute to an unknown sickness, I will have a panic attack. When traveling and sleeping in an unfamiliar bed as well as the unknown in general, a panic attack will also try its hand. And so, I carefully avoid the situations that I am in control of. And for those I am not, I have rehearsed internal pep talks to ward them off.

At the same time panic was introduced into my life, I had my first vasovagal episode. If you're anything like my sister Angee, who responded, "What's wrong with your private parts now?" when I first told her about it, I'll explain myself with further detail.

In basic terms, a vasovagal episode is a fainting episode caused by a drop in blood pressure. My blood pressure has always been pretty low, but I've never fainted or come near to fainting prior to then.

One evening while my children were asleep, I began attempting to clean up some of the disaster of that day. Getting out the vacuum, I decided to first work on common areas, starting with the hall. Almost as soon as I turned the vacuum on, I nearly hit the floor. With my vision going dim and my body experiencing something I had never experienced before, I fought to remain conscious long enough to make it to my couch.

Lying there, I tried to calm down, but I was already dripping with sweat. I was alone with my children as usual. I thought whatever this was would pass, until my hands started contracting.

Twisting inward like a skeletal hand in a haunted house, I did not have control over my fingers anymore. I was losing feeling in my hands, and they would not open back up even by the external physical force of prying them against rigid objects.

I freaked out and called my mom. She had just gotten back home to North Carolina after having been with Paula in Indiana for the past couple of weeks. I could tell she was tired, frustrated, and did not want to deal with this. I would normally just let it go, and even though I felt guilty by needing her help, I was too panicked and scared to handle this one on my own. So, she came over and took me, along with my kids, to the emergency room.

I can't help thinking by her visible annoyance that she felt like this was a false attempt at attention. Maybe she thought since Paula was sick that I wanted to pretend to be too. I don't know. That's all just speculation. I am confident she thinks things like that about me sometimes, so I'm probably not too far off.

The emergency room visit went as always: check-in, wait forever in the lobby, go to triage, then go back out to the lobby and wait forever. Finally, get called back to a room and wait forever once again. You get the gist.

In the end, the doctor explained the vasovagal episode and helped me to understand the whys and possible hows to prevent them.

I believe this incident compounded with my newfound anxiety to make my fear of foreign physical ailments all the worse.

During the follow-up with my primary doctor, he told me to increase the salt in my diet. I thought he was a quack. However, other medical personnel have retold this instruction several times since, so I accept it as sound medical advice. They also told me to flex my calf muscle to keep my blood from pooling in my extremities when I'm standing for long periods of time, as well as to watch my caffeine intake. The latter is an impossibility, but I do tippy-toe exercises during church or while standing in long lines.

✳✳✳

lunchbreak

two grilled chicken sandwiches
mine with extra pickles
sit waiting upon my arrival
the manager gives me a smile
and fresh fries
because I am late
to meet my aunt
who never knew it was that bad
who has come to atone
for the sins of our family

salt rains
on my paper wrapper
the sound of a hundred granules
poured over
racist hurts   mental illness   abuse
I hear my mother read
the Holy Bible
35 years past, searching
for the truth
the parallels between
my grandfather and grandmother

I am reminded of your sincere faith,
which first lived in your grandmother
and in your mother, I am persuaded,
now lives in you

napkins disintegrate
in my clenched fist
as she confirms the atrocities
only my subconscious
has ever acknowledged
we blame Vietnam
or the devil
for my father's transgressions

my body peels away
from the booth
itchy from eyes and ears
felt over our painful words
our actions of solace
half an hour has come
has gone
I shove my sandwich
still whole
and wet from the extra pickles
back into the bag
rise to hug her
never knowing what
occasion will bring us back
together

my breath condenses
a miniature cloud
between my face
and the windshield
I drive back to work with vents aimed
blast the A/C
into my unblinking eyes

Throughout my sister's illness, my mom was my main source for updates on her health. These calls were mostly reassuring. Paula was doing fine, and my mom was investigating alternative treatments for my sister. There were centers in California and Mexico that were looking like viable options.

Setting my phone down after one of these good reports, my phone almost instantly rang again. Assuming my mom forgot to tell me something, I picked it back up and instead saw my sister Angee's number on the screen.

"You need to come now," she said almost as soon as I got out my "hello."

"Wait, what? I just talked to mom, and she specifically told me not to come. That Paula would be going to Mexico soon for some specialized treatment."

"Paula's not traveling anywhere, and you need to get up here right away."

My heart fell to the bottom of my stomach. The urgency in her voice told me all my worst fears were coming true.

Oh God! I needed to pack now. And tell my kids' teachers they would have to miss school. And notify my job. Would my car make it for the trip? Should I try to borrow someone else's? Oh my God, my poor sister! Was she actually dying? Why else did Angee, backed by Charity in the background, sound so aggressive in her demand for my immediate presence?

I'd have to leave on Saturday, Valentine's Day. Thankfully, one of the only cousins I had locally was willing to make the drive with me back home. She would go to visit her mother, father, and brothers in Kentucky, and I would go on a little farther to Indiana.

Not being close to any of my cousins, this trip could have been horribly awkward. But the preoccupation of my mind kept me from noticing any uncomfortable silences that normally would have done all the preoccupying. I know we didn't talk much, and I don't remember a lot from the trip except for trying to hide my tears when I began wondering what I would find upon my arrival.

∗

Unloading the car and taking my bags into Charity's house felt like just another holiday, but this time, the air wasn't alight with the anticipation of feasts or presents. Our kids were still all overjoyed to see each other—the way they always were before their welcome had worn out and they no longer wanted to share toys or couch space with each other. Pausing for a moment, I relished in their unbridled energy as they took off running in the direction of great fun without any ceremonious greetings. I knew that none of them really understood what grave thing brought us unseasonably together in the middle of February.

My sister's house was beautiful. It had two stories and a basement, which I scarcely see anymore, living in a state built on top of red clay. I miss basements. We always had them growing up. The first basement I remembered was in our duplex on Camelot Drive in Grand Rapids, Michigan. The duplex was really only two bedrooms, but with Paula and Charity occupying the top floor's official bedrooms, Lance and I sharing a pullout couch in the living room, and my parents converting the entire basement into their room, we made it work. The next basement I remember was really for us kids. This one was in our ranch home on Heathcliff Drive, also in GR, which was like winning the lottery. For one, I was no longer sharing a sofa bed with my brother, and more importantly, I finally had my own room.

My mother put the most beautiful wallpaper in our formal sitting room that you entered as soon as you came through the front door. It was thick to the touch and covered in lush-looking burgundy flowers with just a hint of greenery. My parents got us a basketball goal in the driveway, and in the backyard was the pièce de résistance: a glorious in-ground pool with a diving board and separate hot tub. It was fenced in and had a bit of yard around the perimeter. There was even enough space for a garden. My mom grew her own bell peppers and tomatoes out there. I'm sure she planted other things, but I'm not sure if they ever actually sprouted. Here was the home where my father brought us our first real pet. A little Lhasa Apso named Shorty Cooper. Shorty could be mean and bit countless people. But he was loved, particularly by Lance, who cared for him up until his death that past fall at seventeen years old—119 in dog years.

By the time we moved to Heathcliff, Paula had graduated high school and was on the first thing smoking back to Kentucky where she would stay in a room in our Mammaw's basement. But in our palace basement was a large family room where Lance and I watched, and also starred in, our own countless movies. There was a large space next to the TV area that had a bathroom and separate entrance to the house that was turned into Charity's refuge. Unfortunately for her, behind her room was another large, empty industrial-looking area that doubled as storage, sometimes an office, and also the most awesome playroom a kid could ever ask for with an uncovered concrete floor that made roller skating inside the house possible.

Charity stayed in Michigan in this house even after the rest of us moved to North Carolina when I was eleven years old. She was a senior in high school and was going to stay behind to graduate and make a life on her own. I know she was glad to be free of us. Each of us for different reasons. She stayed in Grand Rapids, got married, had her children, and worked an amazing job. Here she lived until years later when she packed up her family to move to Indiana and meet Paula who was also moving her family there from Kentucky. They were meeting in the middle, with the plan being to eventually get all of us back up there. When Lance and his new bride made their way back from England to Indiana, it nearly worked out that way— until Paula got sick.

Charity's Indiana house with the basement was homey with rooms to spare. I liked going there. The only thing I didn't like was the cat. Don't get me wrong. I like cats very much and wish I could have one of my own. But I'm allergic to them, and my eyes get itchy along with annoying bouts of sneezing and completely congested airways. Luckily, her cat was an indoor/

outdoor cat, and it usually took me a few days before I couldn't stand it anymore. If anything, I planned on using the cat as an excuse if my eyes were puffed up from any secret crying I had done.

***

Once the kids were settled with Charity keeping watch, I got in the car with Eric (Charity's husband) and Angee.

"Do not look afraid when you see her."

Angee's warning that broke our silence did nothing to calm my nerves.

"When was the last time you've seen Paula?" Eric chimed in.

When I told him it hadn't been since Christmas, his eyes enlarged in the "Oh, shit" kind of way, and he shook his head.

Angee doubled down on her threat with outright sternness, "Just act normal and do not act crazy."

I wish I had the words to describe the terror that was mounting inside of me. I guess it boiled down to fear of the unknown really, and by their reactions, there was much to fear.

The fear made me almost able to forget about the mountain we would drive up to get to Paula's house. Calling it a mountain may be technically incorrect; however, for all intents and purposes, to me it was a mountain. It was a mountain with steep and unsafe cliffs. It was a mountain of which falling off would result in a long and bumpy way down.

She always liked living on top of scary mountains. I never saw the appeal, but that may be due to my fear of falling. I only discovered this fear the one and only time in my life that I had been able to make that cross-country trip to visit Angee in California.

While myself and most of my siblings bounced between Kentucky, Michigan, and North Carolina (moving as my father's job transferred him), Angee pretty steadily stayed in California. Seeing her twice in the span of a couple months was something none of us were used to. We were all glad to have her, the reason why just really sucked.

She did live in the yellow house with us in Radcliff, Kentucky through her middle school years. I refer to this house as "the yellow house" because I was only almost four when we moved from it, and that is how my preschool mind still recalls it.

At the yellow house, Angee, or Icy Ang, and Paula, or Foxy Roxy, (as they were known in their coming of age rap group, The Tender Ladies), lived alongside myself (the baby), Lance (only eighteen months my senior), Charity (who always found herself in an odd "middle child" role stuck between the older, cool kids and "the kids," me and Lance), and my parents.

At some point, even my oldest siblings either lived there or at least visited us, as I remember a particular incident of my oldest brother hanging me upside down by my feet. We had all been left in the house alone, and I had begun to choke on apple juice in my sleep. I'm assuming I was left with a bottle or sippy cup full of juice to aid my slumber. Even though I was so young, I remember the bitter sting of the apple juice being expelled from my throat.

Anyway, by the time we moved to Michigan, Angee had gone back to California with her mom, and I only went to visit her just the once. It was after my oldest daughter was born. I had her at sixteen, so I was probably around seventeen or eighteen.

I remember a few things from that trip. One was Angee revealing that she'd tried to get my parents to let me come visit her for many years, to get a larger sense of the world, because she was "afraid that would happen." I know the "that" was my getting pregnant and becoming a teen mom. In retrospect, as an adult, I can now infer all the reasons why she would've been afraid of that. The other thing I remember was the horrid, near vertical, streets in the Bay Area. At the time, Angee lived in Oakland and worked in San Francisco. In these wretched sideways cities, I had the terrible sense that I was going to fall off the face of the earth. Walking up the steep sidewalks, I had the most incredible urge to get down on all fours and crawl to prevent myself from taking a never-ending tumble. It put such a bad taste in my mouth, I was never able to find an affinity for California.

Paula's first married home was on top of a hill (again, more like a mountain, if you ask me). It was in Brandenburg, Kentucky, and you had to take the narrowest, curviest, continually elevating maze of roads to get to an area that looked like no homes should be put there. Then you parked on this awful patch of not quite gravel, not quite dirt. A plain wooden post was the only barrier to keep you from going a bit too far and driving yourself irreparable over the wrong side of the hill.

Once parked, you had to take a short hike down a steep, inconsistent path of steps to get to the house itself. The home was quaint and comfortable, and once my sister got her hands on it, the interior was made modern and stylish.

While the inside was perfectly fine, once you made it inside, it was the getting there that was so problematic for me. Particularly in the winter, when the maze to get to the house was treacherous, not to mention the parking and walking down those steps, all I could envision was taking an icy slip and tumbling all the way down into the Ohio River that flowed beneath it.

Her current home did not overlook a river, but it was just as scary to get to—more winding little roads with scarce barriers to prevent our car from spilling over the edge.

As we rolled our way higher and higher, we came to the area of road that is often closed in the winter. When the snow and ice were most brutal, a long metal arm would be swung shut, warning drivers that this route was considered too dangerous and was off limits. When it was closed, you'd need to take the long way around, which was a more gradual climb up the mountain that I never got familiar enough with to find on my own, or believe me, I would've.

We were in luck. The weather had been mild enough that the metal gate did not greet us. We continued up the winding way, coming to a curve where the earth and rock soared up one side of the car, and the precipitous drop into a ravine offered itself on the other side.

This stretch reminded of several holidays prior where I found myself in the passenger seat of Paula's car. She saw my eyes widen and my hand grip the door's handle as she raced up the road, barely lowering her speed.

She looked over at me and said, "What's the matter?" with a mischievous laugh that confirmed she knew full well what the matter was.

"I just don't understand why you always want to live up on these insane hills!"

Making the final ascent to where the road leveled off, Eric turned the car right, then left into her neighborhood.

With the car turned off and the keys taken out of the ignition, I did not move. I wanted to remain calm, but my breaths were too shallow and my body trembled. Eric and Angee both paused before exiting the car and went inside. After many moments, with one big swinging effort, I hoisted myself up and out.

I let the frigid winter air rush over me and was proud of this progress, but I could not go in yet. Instead, I walked to a nook in the house between the garage and the elevated walkway that led to the front door. Sitting with my back against the brick, my breaths began to shorten. Barely making its way inside my body before being expelled back out, the air around me began to swirl. I was hyperventilating.

I'm not sure how long this lasted, but Angee made her way back outside and sat with me without words. I knew it was time to pull it together, and after a while, I was able to control my breathing and wiped my face. I had to go in. I had to see my sister no matter what.

Walking into her house was different that time. I had walked in and out of her doors so many times, so easily, so sure. Coming inside now, I walked up the few steps it took to a point where her kitchen, living room, and the door to her master bedroom could be taken in with one grand view.

Before I made it to the top step, I saw her, and I sensed the panic rising again like a twenty-foot wave inside my chest.

I knew she had lost her hair, but I wasn't prepared to see her bald head look so awkward and large sitting atop the frail form not belonging to my sister. This silhouette of a body was cloaked in a matronly zip-up blue robe that also looked like something that could not have belonged to her. Not my beautiful sister.

The noise of my entrance did not stir her to look in my direction, and she just kept shuffling single-mindedly through her kitchen toward the living room with slow, otherworldly footsteps. I wasn't ready for this. They had all tried to warn me, but nothing could have primed me for such a wicked and cruel transformation. I felt I had just seen her a short time ago, normal and whole.

I wanted to turn back around and run out the front door, back to my spot by the garage and resume hyperventilating. My sister Angee had been harsh when she told me not to look afraid when I saw Paula, but now I wasn't sure I'd be able to control the dismay the sight of her had caused me. I don't know if Angee saw the flight plans in my eyes, but she was also stern in telling me to get up the stairs and into the living room.

Paula was now settled in the bend of her enormous sectional. The huge couch made her look even tinier as she sat perched on the edge.

Since Christmas, the cancer had ravaged her body. She was a history textbook photo come to life. Withered away to mirror the emaciated victims of the Holocaust who haunted my middle and high school years, she was a mere physical fraction of the person I had seen just a little over a month ago. Her perfectly white teeth were rotting out of her mouth. Her beautiful blonde hair just scant wisps atop her round head. Her perpetually sun-kissed skin, sallow and waxy. The bone structure, which used to tout her beauty, jutted out mercilessly beneath her thin skin.

With my heart pounding and my breathing uncontrolled again, I rounded the end of the couch as slow as I could without announcing obvious apprehension to the entire room. Oh God, how can they have expected me to act normal when I was in the middle of some grotesque nightmare? My poor, poor sister.

She sat staring straight ahead and appeared to not be entirely aware of her surroundings. However, the movement I was making in her peripheral view must have broken her attention, and she turned only her head toward me.

When our eyes connected, I fought to hold back my tears. I wanted to hold them back for her. I didn't want her to know how scared or how sad I was, especially because she was being so brave. Sometimes bravery can be ridiculous and overrated. Her body was being destroyed, and she should have been able to cry out, plead for help, and beg for mercy without a second thought. But she didn't. Then again, that was never her style anyway.

With a concerted effort to look directly at me, she said, "Hey" casually and then just as slowly as she had turned it toward me, she turned her head back and looked straight ahead at the wall in front of her. Her husband, Ray, must have been used to this reaction from people, or he just expected it from me because he came into the room set to diffuse the shock and silence.

"Why don't you help her eat something?"

He handed me a single-serve container of blueberry yogurt. I hated yogurt, even the smell, but I knew by her eighty-pound frame that she desperately needed to give her body any type of nutrition it would tolerate. Taking the container, my fingers were clumsy and felt large as I fumbled to pull back the top covering. I panicked for a second, not knowing if I needed to spoon-feed her bites, or whether she could still do it herself. I knew everyone was watching me. By now, my mom and Angee had also joined us in the living room. Panicking, my eyes bolted around the room from face to face, but there was no time or way to ask what I was supposed to do. Dipping the spoon into the purplish cream, I collected a tiny portion on the tip and brought it shaking to her lips. With still, slow motions, Paula took the spoon from me and resumed feeding herself without a word. Knowing I had probably embarrassed her by denying her this simple dignity, I felt like a jackass and just sat there. I didn't know where to look. It was entirely too uncomfortable to just stare at Paula taking minuscule bits of yogurt, so after giving Ray a smile meant to say, "This is no biggie; I can handle it," I decided to stare at the wall too.

After two bites and a sip of water, she was finished. This made my stomach drop. Two tiny bites of yogurt were all she could muster. In less than ten minutes, she wound up throwing this up too.

My mom took our gathering as an opportunity to rally the idea of Paula flying out west to be healed at an alternative treatment center.

This was her final effort to grasp onto this delusion. However, the level of certainness and severity may have varied, but there was a resounding and collective "no way" from all assembled.

At this point, it was clear Paula had held on because she knew we couldn't let her go. Though she was uncomfortable, miserable, and suffering, she endured it as long as she had because she felt obligated to live and continue fighting, and in turn, suffering for us.

"This is not my decision. It affects all of you." The words were severed from each other as if the cancer had crawled up into her throat and had choked them one by one. The statement came out quiet, but not soft.

But this was her decision entirely, and we assured her of that. We would not subject her to this last bit of torture to satisfy our own selfishness. She had fought gallantly these past two months. Initially, I'm sure for her own self. After all, most people want to live. Though I suspect after a while, her willingness to continue undergoing treatments was strictly for us, her family. But she was tired now, and we reassured her it was okay for her to finally rest.

Knowing she was outnumbered, my mother went from being the confident spokesperson heading up this cause, well-researched and knowledgeable, to being outright deflated. She no longer had any choice but to acquiesce. The detailed orchestration and planning for Paula's recovery filled up her mind to squeeze out the extra space that might have allowed the harsh reality of the situation to seep through. Although she was not the last to know, she was the last to accept what might just be inescapable. I took one look at Paula, and any remaining glimmer of hope that had survived in my mind was extinguished. But my mom had assigned herself the role of being my sister's savior in this misfit cast, and though the cruel truth showed itself long before this moment, it took a room full of us to tell her unequivocally that Paula would not survive the travel before she resigned to defeat and surrendered to inevitability.

Without a single movement, Paula sat there and finally resigned herself. She waved the white flag.

***

constellation's concession

my outstretched hand
petite crescent moon
lying on its back
lingers for a while
held up by yearning
and the stars
wearied by wishes
that travel light-years
to reach them
long after the supplicant
turns to dust
and lighted candles
never have a chance
to provide anything more
and grant much less
than the filling
of hollowed spaces
and empty hands

After Paula retired to her room, I planned to pop into the basement to set my bags down. As I was getting ready to descend the stairs, Ray was coming up. We paused for a moment before he asked, "Should I tell the kids?"

Of course, the children knew their mother was ailing, but even up until this moment, no one talked to them about the idea of her actually dying. No one told them how probable, how inevitable—no one told them their mother would soon be gone.

So there we were. Ray, a man who externally looked to have everything under control, asking his wife's baby sister, whom no one deferred to for anything of consequence, something so monumental. He looked vulnerable and in need of guidance, or perhaps what he needed was permission to do an unbearable thing.

Mustering every ounce of confidence and assuredness I could, I answered, "Yes. You should tell them she is dying and, as much as you can, get them ready for when it comes."

Ray seemed to gain just a bit of strength, and with determination, went on to do the thing everyone had avoided. He had maybe the hardest job of all.

In not much time, I worked my way back upstairs and went straight away to Paula's room. I just wanted to be near her.

She appeared to be asleep, and I stood a few feet from the side of her bed, watching her. Her body was so tiny and looked so fragile, and I just stared.

"What?" she said, startling me out of my trance. I had assumed she was fast asleep, but she had been watching me look at her. I was embarrassed and turned my head to face the window while she drifted back to sleep.

This went on for hours. I just hovered around her, rarely leaving the room while she slept. But as the day progressed, her level of consciousness rapidly declined. She was taken, with assistance, to the bathroom a couple times, and this aroused her awareness for a moment. But mostly she was only there in body. The Paula that was on the couch feeding herself yogurt just hours before was already gone.

When she was tucked back into bed, she looked to be gone again. I sat on the edge near her, lost in thought. Suddenly, Paula arose, almost to the point of sitting.

"Oh, it's you. Hey," and she gave me a hug as if seeing me there for the first time. Just as quickly, she went back down on the bed and back to her state of semi-consciousness.

These pops of awareness happened less and less and occurred just a few more times that day. They were always unexpected, but it was nice to have her return to us, if only for a couple of seconds.

Eventually, my oldest daughter, Jazlyn, had been summoned to the house to say goodbye to her aunt. My younger two were just three and five years old, and the sight of their aunt as she was then would be too much for them. I didn't want that to be their lasting memory of her. But Jaz was ten. Ten years of summer and holiday visits, ten years of family vacations, ten years of the aunt she knew and adored. She deserved to see her again, no matter how hard it would be.

There is no preparing a child for how cancer changes a person. Hell, there's no preparing an adult. When she burst into tears at the sight of my sister, it was heartbreaking, but expected.

Paula fortunately did not appear to be aware enough to be upset by Jazlyn's reaction, and by the time she made her way to the bed, Jaz began to compose herself, and her tears became silent.

Once again, the switch was flipped, and Paula came back to us. She lit up like Christmas at the sight of my daughter. She recognized her as soon as she opened her eyes, and Jazlyn got to hug her beloved aunt one more time. When Jazlyn left the room, so did Paula's cognizance.

The life of this day was enough to fill months upon months. Family members streamed into my sister's room one by one, each taking a turn as if waiting in line for an amusement park ride. Everyone had come to see her one last time. I couldn't be sure who had summoned them all there. It probably would not have been my mother. Perhaps Ray. He would have found it a meaningful responsibility needing to be done and tackled it accordingly. Either way, they were all there, and I would have rather them not been.

Seldom having moved from my post next to my sister's bed since my arrival, I remained seated beside her as the visitors filed in. Cousins, aunts, and neighbors came bearing their grief, but I wanted none of it. Keep your tears and your sadness. She's my sister, not yours. She's my mother's daughter, not yours. She's my nieces' and my nephews' mom, not yours. Their presence reeked of obligation, and they were wasting time. And with hope relinquished, time was the only thing we had left.

Analyzing each entrant, my eyes were fixed upon the doorway as my Mammaw came in to see her granddaughter for the last time. I had never fully gotten used to seeing her with an entire head full of bright white hair. After decades of dying it a dark brown that hinted more toward black, she had given up this vanity at the urging of one of my older aunts. My aunt had gone gray without a fight and pressed her mother to do the same. Seeing her enter my sister's home, I imagined those short white tufts of hair being as soft to the touch as a newborn lamb's fleece, framing the face of a living angel.

Walking toward me, I got myself on my feet and geared up to receive her ever-intense embrace. These are mighty hugs meant to convey every ounce of her love in a physical instance. Without hesitation, she pulled me close to her, and my body went all but limp. The firmness of anger from all these intruders released its hold on me as my muscles relaxed and my knees nearly disappeared. Silently sobbing into her thick sweater, she pulled me away from her and looked into my face.

"She needs to go home now."

Nodding with no words, I agreed. I knew the end was approaching, and she could and would leave us at any moment.

Leaving me standing, Mammaw walked over to the other side of Paula's bed. By now, my sister had been laid on her side and was facing the bedroom window, though whatever was in her line of sight must have been a million miles in the distance. Her consciousness and awareness had continued to diminish greatly throughout that day, and she showed no physical reaction to the presence of any of the earlier visitors, save my daughter.

But as Mammaw approached her, Paula woke up from whatever place she had been off visiting and reached out for her. Delicately, but with a swift confidence, Mammaw wrapped her arms around my sister's fragile body, and I knew she was saying goodbye.

**

Once everyone but our immediate family was gone, Angee joined my bedside vigil.

"So, what's up? Just hanging out with Paula?"

"Yeah," my voice came out smaller than I intended.

Angee smiled and said, "Yeah, she's pretty great, huh?

We sat at the foot of the bed talking in venerated tones of our sister's magnificent character as an intentional shift from the more depressing direction our conversation could've taken.

Cutting through a moment of silence, Paula's small voice spoke out.

"Look out for them."

As she had been without speech and seemingly without consciousness for some time now, this sudden outburst of speech shocked me. The look of confusion on Angee's face echoed my own.

"Who, Paula?" I asked.

"Them out there."

And without further explanation, we knew exactly who "they" were. She was having us make a promise. One we made to her while she was on her deathbed. This meant she knew she was not going to be around much longer. This meant soon she'd be dead. She was asking us to look out for the most precious thing she had. She was asking us to look out for her children. "We will" was all we could manage to choke out. Both of us refreshed with a new round of tears that we wouldn't dare let her see or hear.

❈

As the evening wore on, Ray came in the bedroom ready for sleep. This meant my time with Paula was up, so down I went to join Angee in the basement. I promised her I would do her hair, so we whipped out the flatiron and all the necessary products to begin.

It's funny how you can collectively make believe that something horrible isn't happening right above you because there's nothing else you can do. In this fashion, Angee and I discussed my time being locked up in the mental institution.

"We are all our own special freak show," Angee assured me. That's for damn sure.

"Yeah, Lance tried to convince me that I should've called dad while I was in there. But that would've been suicide."

We both laughed at my sophomoric joke. Egged on, I continued.

"I'd sooner die than go back to that place!" We laughed harder. "I fought like 'crazy' to get out."

While we were doubled over in a fit of giggles by our goofy dark humor, my mom popped down for just a second to tell us there was some food left from earlier if we were hungry. Just as quick, she went back up to the kitchen where she was avoiding sleep by either cleaning or cooking more food.

Then it happened.

Ray came down the stairs, and he told us—during the few short moments that he had left their room to check something in the kitchen, Paula had left this world.

I couldn't help but believe that she was so intentional in this act. We had not left her alone all day long. Someone was by her side constantly. Then, the first moment she was finally and completely alone, she left for good. Her final deed was one of graciousness.

Wearied anew, Angee and I carried our tired, sorrowed bodies back up the stairs and into Paula's room. My mom was already there. She looked years more exhausted than just fifteen minutes ago.

"Well, she's at peace now. I guess it's over." And with that, her and Ray left the room to call hospice and arrange the things no one ever wants to have to arrange for someone they love.

Angee and I were alone in the room. Just us and what remained of our sister.

Pulling back the covers, I did what I had wanted to do all day. With a small bounce, I pushed myself onto the high bed and lay next to her. Holding her still hands, I took her in. I knew it wouldn't be long until even her body would be removed from us forever. So, I just lay there and hung onto my big sister.

Though there were innumerable tears before this moment and the future would hold just as many if not more, right then and there none of us cried. She didn't get a chance to fight long, but she fought hard. She deserved peace, and I believe it's true what they say—we knew she was in a far better place.

A rapping on the front door broke the silence that was occupying the house. Hospice had arrived to help in these final moments. Angee and I stayed put in silence, and we listened to the conversation happening in the next room.

The hospice lady was assisting my mom with the funeral arrangements, and the folks from the funeral home in Brandenburg would arrive shortly. I could hear my mom begin listing all those who had survived Paula, and as she got to our siblings, the woman interrupted her.

"So, are these foster children?"

Not understanding the question, my mom gave her a slow "No" as a reply. She continued listing myself and my brother and sisters and was interrupted again.

"Why do they have different last names?"

"They're grown and have married names" was my mom's answer, which wasn't entirely true. Our complicated family tree jutted askew branches in unorthodox directions, but the answer was true enough for the dummy asking those ridiculous questions at a time like this.

"Amateurs!" Angee muttered. "They sent us amateurs!"

The inevitable came, and Paula's body went. We left each other and retreated to our separate corners of the house alone. I never did finish Angee's hair.

∗∗∗

an alarm clock rings

today arms
at awkward angles
blistering smells
hair pried apart
a decade of ache
in one inch of muscle
taut black gauze
bubbled over flesh
covers eyes

I cling
to yesterday's colors
mirrors
that whispered
my name

The gravel crunched beneath my tires as I parked on the side of a building that sat off one of the only main roads the town of Brandenburg had. My hand lingered on the gearshift long after the car had been put into park. I looked down to examine what I was wearing once more: a brown and cream, diagonally plaid shirt with an open collar and three oversized faux buttons going down my chest and flat, metal, teal earrings with hints of gold that dangled and eventually twisted themselves the wrong way. I expected the people inside the funeral home would consider my earrings large. I considered them small. My pants were dark brown and boring. I figured I could wear them again for work. Going to a funeral home dressed fully as myself just didn't seem quite proper. I needed to project respectability, and greater than that, I needed to blend in.

The pep talk that circled round my head wouldn't make a bit of sense if I tried to lay it all out here linearly. Getting myself to move out of the car proved to be a deed much more difficult than I'm sure it looked from the outside. I needed to go in and see my sister. Fuck, I didn't want to see my sister. Not like this. Not in a casket. There's no way to fortify yourself, no words that will make sense of such a task. My sister was dead. My sister is dead. Even years later, I still think these words in my own mind and can't believe they're true.

One way or another, I made it out of the car and walked up the steps all right—almost like going into a dentist's office. But inside, instead of a receptionist desk and uncomfortable seating, there were flowers. Lots of flowers everywhere. And there was a hall with many doors. The doors on the left led to small rooms: offices, a kitchen, a bathroom. But the doors on the right all opened to one big room. A room where my sister lay inside of a box.

There were tables with small yellow sheets of paper throughout the room. They were there for visitors to write memories of my sister. People said some kind things about her. I didn't write anything, though. I couldn't remember anything. Well, I remembered everything, but they were just bits and pieces of a million different stories. I couldn't finish one without another flooding my mind. None of them did her or us any justice. None of them summed up anything about her.

I walked past these tables and made my way to a wooden bench that was smack dab in the middle of the room. I sat there alone. The bench faced my sister's casket, but it was low enough and the casket high enough that I couldn't see her. I couldn't face seeing her yet. Not yet. Jesus, my sister was in a casket.

I sat by myself and tried not to pay too much attention to all the people around me. I wondered if they realized she was my sister. I wondered if they wondered who the hell this strange girl was sitting by herself in the middle of the room. I never lived around there, and no one but my older, less immediate relatives would know me. No one bothered trying to come and make small talk with me. That I am thankful for.

As time drudged on, my favorite cousin, Matlyn, made her way over to me, and she stuck around. Hers was company I could live with. Hers was company I needed.

Throughout the years, she had accumulated numerous tattoos (including one on her head), had any number of piercings and large ear gauges, and her red hair was varying lengths and cuts, ranging from popstar to rocker to halfway shaved off her head. Young children and old strangers alike often misinterpreted her gender.

My dear Matlyn was more than ten years younger than me, but I've always had a kindred connection with her. Even though we grew up so many states away and didn't have a close familial union, somehow she found her way to me during her teenage years. She struggled with her mental health and her worthiness, and I ached for her. Feeling alone and misunderstood was something I knew well.

She sat on the bench next to me, and instead of offering solemn condolences or a peppy cheer-up speech, she made me laugh. That is her far underutilized gift. Her apt storytelling and comedic timing came off in a way that you'd question whether she even realized she was being funny. But it was, indeed, intentional.

She began by telling me she had visited her grandmother (her father's mother, so no relation to me) earlier that day. Her grandmother hadn't realized it was Matlyn until she got a look at her rear end. The idea of being recognized only by her butt tickled me, and so I laughed. Loud. I was laughing and could not stop laughing, right in the middle of my sister's wake.

But as all good things come to an end, Matlyn wandered off to talk to her mom. Finding myself alone once more, I took the moment to pick up my phone and dialed Paula's number. It rang a few times and then went to voicemail. "Hello, you've reached Paula. Please leave a message...." I hung up and called it again and listened to her voice come through the phone. I soaked in the tone and all the little inflections: the way the ending "a" in Paula went up an octave, hinting at her southern twang. I would never have a conversation with my sister again, and I needed to memorize her voice.

But what if I couldn't? What if it was lost forever? What if I couldn't even remember my own sister's voice? These are the things you panic about after death that nobody even knows to warn you of. "Hello, you've reached Paula." To this day, those four words are the only ones I can hear her saying in my head. Everything else is just silence.

I put my phone away, and with a sudden burst of determination, I swung my body forward, planted my feet on the ground, and stood up from the bench. I would go visit my sister for a bit. I walked alone to the casket. The people who had been viewing her finally left, and I could have her by myself for a few moments.

The smell preserving her was overwhelming, but she looked a lot more like herself than she had in the days prior. The mortician did a pretty decent job. The wig they put on her was a nice color, but still a wig. I found out later that one of my other little cousins did her makeup. I think Paula would've liked that.

She was wearing a bracelet Maggie had made her: pink beads, pink flip-flop charm, blue purse charm, and a heart for the clasp. They had managed to change her hands from the purple they had turned back to flesh color. They were so cold, but I grabbed and held onto them anyway.

I could see the adhesive where her lips had been glued together, and I couldn't help myself from imagining that Paula would have been so pissed by this.

At that moment, I just wanted to crawl in the casket with her and go to sleep.

A queue began to form behind me, and I knew my time with my sister was up. I made my way to the kitchen, which became the holding area for everyone who needed a break from the actual wake itself. My mother, brother, sisters, cousins, aunts, uncles, nieces, nephews, and my own children rotated in and out. There were snacks and drinks a plenty, which were always a welcome distraction.

I took a seat in one of the empty chairs and was soon joined by Lance and Angee. Our usual lighthearted banter turned to death and yet still managed to remain lighthearted all the same. I suppose it's safe to say in our family, we make jokes to cope with pain.

"If I die, you guys can just cremate me into a keychain. That way each of you will always have me with you," Angee suggested.

"No, I'll put my portion into a Boggle hourglass, and you can still join us when we play board games," Lance replied.

"I can see it all now," I said. "One of my kids will end up breaking it, and Angee's ashes will be everywhere. 'Damnit, Zipporah! Is that Aunt Angee on your pants?'"

We laughed, and we kept ourselves laughing until we couldn't. Pulled apart by another family member, or the call of nature, or the need for solitude and introspection, we disbanded, and I found myself wandering the large room that contained Paula's remains yet again.

From some unseen speakers overhead, music had been playing on constant rotation throughout the wake. I learned later that Ray had burned a disc with some of Paula's favorite songs. Rob Thomas, Keith Urban, Earth Wind and Fire, and Jason Mraz sang and sang and sang. I stayed with Paula as those songs serenaded my grief for what felt like all day. In reality, it was about seven or eight hours.

For months to come, whether on the radio or playing in the back of a TV commercial, I couldn't bear to hear any of those songs and would snap them off in an instant.

But whenever they come on now, I pretend it's my sister stopping by to say hello.

***

The next day was the funeral. I mentally armed myself, determined to make it through the forthcoming events as emotionally unscathed as possible. I didn't want to cry anymore. After spending the entire previous day at her wake, I was depleted.

The service would start at two p.m. at Brandenburg United Methodist Church. That meant a morning with enough hours to eat breakfast, get my kids dressed, remember my sister's dead, get myself dressed, position my car in the caravan of vehicles that would trek the hour from Indiana back down to Kentucky, all while remembering my sister was dead.

The church's exterior was all white with a gray roof and a singular steeple. A couple of wooden doors allowed you inside, but the interior details are a blur. There were probably pews. Probably beautiful flowers. I'd like to make believe there were stained glass windows. I find stained glass tends to elevate most occasions, but to be honest, I can't be sure.

I kept Paula's funeral program in hand throughout the service for frequent reference. I needed to know where we were at all moments, to work through keeping my emotions in check. Only five more things to get through. Two more songs. One more prayer, and so on.

The Christmas before Paula got sick, it was business as usual. We drove up to see her in Indiana, and while there, the two of us did some Christmas shopping. At the mall one city over, we perused the shops with Paula doing most of the buying. After picking up some bedding and other odds and ends, we moseyed into the type of store that sells scented lotions and candles.

She went in and straightaway found what she was looking for. After making the purchase, she handed the bag to me. It was a gift.

"Whenever I get stressed teaching school or whatever, I use coconut lime lotion and pretend I'm at the beach."

Since then, I've made it a habit to always have a coconut lotion in my personal stock. I don't know if it's the actual scent, or just the memory, but it helps remarkably in calming me down. I wish I had some now.

My cousin's wife sung one of the songs listed on the agenda. It was beautiful and was something about dancing with angels. She sang in a gorgeous soprano, which I found fitting. I attempted to let the lyrics wash over me without penetration. It mostly worked, and I only had to dab my eyes a few times.

The other musical moment in the program worth mentioning was the playing of Bob Marley's "Three Little Birds." It was apparently one of my sister's favorite songs. I never knew it, but that made sense. Though me and my other sisters often commiserated about our childhood, Paula had some form of amnesia. She just didn't remember all the unpleasant happenings the way that we did. I believe she intentionally forgot them.

I spied Paula's oldest child sitting throughout the service, their face hardened and unmoved, in contrast to Maggie who was nestled under my mom's wing, crying openly. But the moment that is most vivid in my memory is right before her casket was to be closed. That darling child, who braves the world with faux disdain and disinterest, stood on their tippy-toes and bent over their mother to kiss her one last time.

Doug, her first husband and father of her biological children, helped to carry my sister out of the church. I still think of him as my brother, and I found this final act meaningful and kind.

The burial was to take place at St. Mary Magdalene Cemetery in Payneville, KY. All of these rural towns blend one right into another, so I'm not sure when the transition from Brandenburg to Payneville took place. But I did recognize that this was my Mammaw's church, which would wind up being the location for all future Thanksgivings as our large family got too big to fit in her house.

Paula's actual gravesite was going to be down a hill in a patch of land that was a little less crowded with headstones. The weather was approximately either too rainy or snowy. It was gloomy and dangerous enough to prevent us from making it safely down the slope. So, we did not witness her being put in the ground. Instead, a small canvas tent was set over an area of grass at the top of the hill. It was too small to fit all whom were in attendance, so I stayed out from under it and to the back of the crowd. I didn't want to miss what was going on because I needed to keep my eyes on my sister for as long as possible. Soon, that option would never be afforded to me again.

Prior to the funeral, Angee recounted a time when Paula was in the hospital. A time that, even now, enrages me. Angee and Charity had accompanied her, and Ray was there but had stepped out. Paula was visited by a doctor in training, and they made the mistake of asking this clown if there was any hope. He proceeded to cock his head to the side at an attempt of sincerity, but unconvincingly said, "Well, there's always hope. But no one survives at this stage."

"Well then, what's the point?"

Angee told me that when Paula said this, her expression was that of a person who had lost all hope. When Ray came back and saw their faces, he rightfully let those idiots have it. After he complained at the front desk, Paula's original oncologist, who had true compassion, came to talk with them, but the damage was done. When I heard this story, I wish I had been there to bash his face in. Oh, how I wanted to hurt him the way he hurt her. And I wonder if this was the moment her mind, body, and spirit gave up the fight. How can a person go on without hope? Of course, I understood this feeling but in a different way.

As the burial portion of the program wrapped up, there were some sympathetic ceremonial words spoken and corresponding actions taken. But in the end, it was anticlimactic. We were expected to say our amens, turn and walk back to our cars, all while my sister was still lying in that box right in front of us.

The well-worn saying goes that time heals all wounds. I believe that statement excludes the death of someone who has been a part of you. The fresh, raw, all-consuming emotions may fizzle out, but the pain doesn't go away. It changes over time. But it never actually goes away. You will still think right out of nowhere, this cannot be real. They cannot be gone forever. You'll have to replay that fact over again in your head. It will take some convincing, but the truth really is that you will never see them again.

The due you're allotted for grief is a funny thing. Not funny-haha. Rather, funny-annoying. Funny-hurtful. Funny-not enough. It pretty much parallels the moment when you pull away from the cemetery and your car lights are no longer flashing. Nobody stops or gives you the right of way any longer. You get that brief moment to put on your flashers, and everyone pulls over for you to acknowledge your loss. But once your loved one is buried, the world keeps driving on. Right around you, if need be.

Sometimes an imaginary video of Paula plays in my mind over and over again, her stomach exposed—maybe she's wearing a bathing suit, a bikini, and it protrudes in a slightly odd sort of way. She's in great shape, so this protrusion is made to appear even odder. But these are the kinds of thoughts that could drive you crazy; the kinds of thoughts that say, "Hey, maybe if you had looked closer, maybe if had you said something, none of this would have happened." Maybe we were all guilty of ignoring what was there. And maybe my mind and memories are just playing tricks on me.

The words "my sister is dead" still come out of my mouth like vomit. It bubbles up in my throat. The tell-tale salivation starts to collect in my mouth, and then out it comes up without much warning and at inapt times. Sometimes I become so desperate to share this information with anyone with ears that it feels like I must have emotional Tourette's.

Then there are moments of low humanity, when someone, somewhere will just do something stupid to you for no real reason at all with zero consideration or compassion. Maybe someone cuts you off and proceeds to give you the finger. Maybe the cashier huffs and puffs and rolls his eyes while you're struggling to find a couple more coins to finalize your checkout. Or your coworker is trying to get you in trouble for running in a few minutes late for work. In these moments, I want to scream to these rude assholes, "My sister just died! Can't you just be human for a second!"

From passing interactions, some basic humanity is all that's called for. For non-strangers, I'd advise going above this. Whenever you discover that someone you know has a dear family member or friend with a life-threatening illness, offer to come to him or her. I don't think for a minute that everyone must react to this type of news the same way as me, but if there are even some that do, please spare them the devastation of having to digest this kind of news alone. All I can think of is how nice it would be to have another person to talk to, to say this shit is completely unfair. Someone to maybe make you laugh and change the subject for you, so you're not left alone with your thoughts. It's at least worth a shot, and the worst they can say is, "No thanks."

***

Reflection

some look at the time
others the floor
anywhere but at me,
a girl made up of refuse
the spider left behind
still others try to capture
the glint in my eye
blinding like a sword
victorious in battle
I check the floor
for unevenness
look at the time
anywhere but at the girl
inside the mirror's cracks

The first dream happened shortly after that terrible, horrible, no good, very bad day: February 16, 2009. It had to have been the second or third week after I returned home. I went to sleep that evening missing my sister as I had done every night and every day before.

After having drifted off, I found myself back in my sister's home in Indiana. It wasn't the same house, though. Not the same layout or furniture, but I knew it was supposed to be her home, nonetheless. My mom was there as well as my sister, Charity. Ray and Trey (Ray's son, who was as good as her own) were also in the house but not in the same room with us. I didn't see them or hear them, but in a dream simply knowing something is becomes enough.

The three of us were trying on Paula's clothes and deciding how to best distribute it all. Standing around in her closet trying on skirts and hats seems like a stupid thing to be doing after what just happened. But I tried not to judge my dreamself too harshly for participating because I've found that any activity that served as a distraction was pretty much okay in my book.

Just as we were each going around trying on a pair of blue heels, she appeared. Even in the dream, it wasn't her flesh-and-blood-self. She was more of an apparition.

"They don't suit any of you."

I don't remember my sister ever using phrases with "suit" in that context before, but she definitely had no qualms telling us when she thought something we were wearing was not so hot, so this wasn't out of character for her at all.

"I miss you."

That was me talking to her this time.

"I miss you too." That was her.

I hugged her, and then she just sort of faded away. The dream ended after that.

The next dream happened later that year. It was in the fall, Halloween night to be exact, though I don't believe the day had any relevance.

This time I was alone, and I was in a room that had no walls. Even though the room seemed infinite, in the center of the room, there was a small round table with a black kettle phone sitting on it. There were two white armchairs placed on either side of the table. I was sitting in one of the chairs, and the second was empty.

I don't remember the phone ringing and me picking it up. I also don't remember me dialing out and waiting for someone to answer. Nevertheless, I was on the phone, and I knew right away who was on the other end. I was talking to my sister, and she was still dead.

Desperation and urgency flooded my mouth, and words came flying out, "I miss you. I want to see you. I want to touch you. I want to hug you."

My sister didn't say much, but her voice was just as desperate and just as urgent. But it was a different type of desperation and a different type of urgency than mine. I think what made it different was the frustration in her voice. She wanted to hear me, and she understood. But there was something she needed me to understand too, and she knew it was partially my fault that I didn't because I didn't want to understand it.

"You do see me."

That's what she said, and she said it over and over again.

"You do see me. You *do* see me."

In the background, I could hear that there was something going on, but it sounded so far away. It was the sound of people and their activity. Wherever she was, there was something magnificent happening. I could tell because besides the desperation, urgency, and frustration in her tone, there was also eagerness. It was as if she had stepped away from something important. Something she didn't want to be away from. Something she was in a rush to get back to.

"I have to go."

She hung up, and I woke up. My cheeks were wet. I had been crying in my sleep.

There is one more dream that I had of her, and it was in between the two I've already shared. Paula was sick, but she was still alive. This is a key point to remember. She was *still alive*. I was in Florida and driving on a highway. I have no idea why I or she, for that matter, would have been in Florida. The only times we were ever there together in real life was when we went to Disney World a couple times while I was in elementary school and once when I just started college. But in this dream, we were not going to visit Mickey Mouse.

Okay, so I was driving on the highway, and I was talking on my cell phone. Yeah, I know I was on the phone again, but this time I wasn't talking to Paula. She was never really present in the dream. I knew she was "around," but I never actually saw her or talked to her. That is another important thing to take note of. I think she was in some special hospital, which was the reason we were in Florida, and I was on the phone talking to her doctor.

The doctor was telling me that I was a compatible donor. What I'd be donating, I had no clue. My dreamself must have known because I didn't ask for clarification. All I knew was that she needed something for an experimental procedure, and I was elated by this good news of me being a match.

The dream was over shortly after this, and I woke up. Because of the excitement and hope this faux phone call aroused, I had to remind myself that there was indeed no such hope. My sister would not be cured because my sister was already dead. This part especially sucked.

Here's the thing, in the first two dreams, that *was* my sister. Not like, yeah, it was the sound of her voice, or yeah, it was how she looked, but it was actually *her*. As in, she came and she visited me in these dreams—her actual self or her soul or whatever—it was *her*. I know I'm being a bit repetitive, but I want you to see the point, so you're clear about what I'm saying. My sister came back to me because she knew I needed her.

The state I was in during the time of the first dream goes without saying, but I'm gonna say it anyway. I was pitiful. I know everyone was despondent. My sister had been so violently sick and died so fast, and it was all so aching and new. But from my tales of mental instability, you can probably gather on your own that I was in about as fragile a place as a piece of porcelain rocking on the edge of a table during an earthquake. My sister knew this about me. My sister *knows* this about me.

That was her who reassured me that she missed me too in that first dream. It was her I hugged. Not just some imaginary sensation my brain created during REM sleep. The dream that happened next, the Florida dream, was crap. That was all me. How I see it, it was pointless and only made everything worse. I was sad after the others also, but I wasn't angry. I just wanted more of her. That kind of farce Florida dream I wanted no more of whatsoever.

The third dream was her again, but more importantly, it was also God. It was her whom I was talking to on the phone, but it was God who let her (and maybe even told her to) talk to me. I mean, it's really always God, isn't it? But this time it was He who gave her either permission or encouragement (depending on how you look at it) to leave whatever she had been busy doing to comfort me one more time.

However, the haste in which she had gotten off the phone let me know that I shouldn't be expecting her back again anytime soon.

***

142

Kentucky

is 597 miles
beneath my car's tires

Thanksgiving turkeys
and Christmas hams

Mammaw's
concrete embrace

Pappaw's
empty recliner

Aunt and Uncle's tobacco farm
and hearts full of Jesus

Where all street signs read
    Paula

Kentucky

is phone calls that begin with long pauses
and end with bad news

maxed out credit cards for dark clothing
to wear just once

three gray tombstones
in an icy church yard

homes atop rocky hills that crumble
into the Ohio River of my dreams

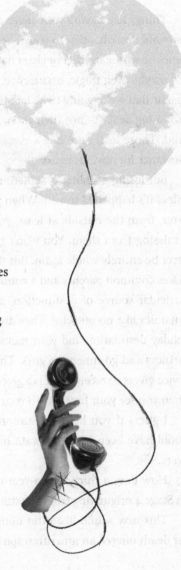

Things like having your sister die of cancer when you're twenty-seven years old don't happen to you. They happen to other people. We all know someone whose brother or sister has died. We know it and accept it as a sad, and maybe even tragic, occurrence, but then we remember our cable bill is due, or that we're going to be late to a PTA meeting. After all, it's not really such a big deal. It's not their mom or their spouse, or heaven forbid, their child. Those losses are due a certain amount of respect and a major grief allowance for obvious reasons.

But losing a sibling is something else altogether, and you won't get it unless it's happened to you. When you see people who've lost a brother or sister, from the outside at least, you won't be able to see that something is missing from them. You won't realize from just looking that they will never be entirely whole again. But they won't. They have lost someone who shares common parents and a common history. Someone who knows their particular source of dysfunction, and who understands their stories and dynamics like no one else. They are your children's keepers. They are your holiday destination and your memories. They are your vacation planning partners and go-inners on gifts. They are your role models, your mentees, advice givers or receivers. It is a given that they are part of the future you see when you see your future with your mind's eye.

I guess if you have this unfortunate understanding, these sentences would have been more accurate having used past tenses like "knew" and "were."

How does a thirty-seven-year-old get diagnosed with cancer, find out it's Stage 4 originating from her stomach, and die within two months?

This may sound like utter nonsense or even a tad morbid, but to me, her death offered an unwritten spiritual protection for both myself and the rest of my siblings. Here's how I see it: there is no way God will let me or my brothers or any of my other sisters die young or in too tragic a way. It would be too much for our mother and too much for one another. In this way, I view Paula as a sacrificial lamb.

That's why when my sister Angee was diagnosed with brain cancer the same year of Paula's death, I cried for the pain and battle that was in store for her. Not out of fear that we would lose her. God wouldn't do that to us. He just could not. Those sorts of grotesque tragedies only happen in tearjerker melodramas. I choose to believe they cannot happen in real life. Just the same, I know that every last one of us would take our chances with fate to have her back.

This doesn't shake my faith in God. I'm just not that type of person. I have no need to question, "Why my sister?," "Why now?," or any other type of Why. I'm content with knowing that there is some greater purpose. I don't need the evidence. I don't need to know what good has come from this tragedy. Because there must be a reason, or everything else that goes along with these thoughts is unimaginable. But that doesn't change the fact that my heart is broken and that I'll always have an emptiness inside me with Paula's name on it.

✳✳✳

I am convinced that when you die, your loved ones who have already passed on come back to help you make the transition. Sitting in retrospect, having now watched more than one person I love die, one thing they have in common is that before they go, they always start talking to people who were long dead. Paula started seeing and talking to her father's mother, and my granddad started talking to his baby sisters. I think of all the people who will help me go whenever my time on earth is up.

Sitting in the passenger seat on my way back to North Carolina, I found this thought comforting. My mom was driving with me and my children back home. It was a normal trip in the fact that there were plenty of inconvenient bathroom stops, lots of drinks, snacks, and messes, and the breaking up of fights about every ten minutes of the nine-hour journey. But the weight of the air inside the car was heavier than usual.

Before my abrupt departure to get to my sister, I gave my resignation from my position as a senior center social worker with no plans of returning. Initially, I thought maybe this was my time to move to Indiana and get us one step closer to reuniting as a family geographically. I planned on leaving everything behind to go aid in the care of my sister while she fought on her winding road to recovery. Once those ideas had been dashed by Angee and Charity's frantic phone call, I thought that I'd at least be in Indiana for an extended period of time. I didn't think she'd die almost as soon as I got there. Either way, I had no plans of returning. So now, defeated and dejected, I was going back home to be alone with my three little kids in our cramped apartment without employment. I was too weary to panic, so I didn't even bother to worry about what I'd do next.

My mom was the type of person who could drive for hours with no music on. I'm all for silence and reflection, but when I'm in the car, I want the music up, and I want it loud. During one of these silences, which were really just moments to focus solely on the endless kid requests, messes, and fights, my mom said, "You must really feel crazy," as if noticing this for the first time. "Having you and Lance eighteen months apart really made me absolutely crazy, and I had Charity, Paula, and your dad. You only have Jazlyn, and I know that's hard on her."

It was as if, for the first time, she had a moment's understanding of how challenging my life often was.

"Yeah, I do feel crazy most of the time."

We continued to ride through the hours on a mostly unremarkable trip; however, a loud, unpleasant, and familiar sound broke through a moment of quiet.

"Ewwwww!" two out of my three kids shrieked.

The third, looking quite pleased, could hardly contain a giggle.

We cracked all of the windows, and while my face was still turned in disgust, my mom said, "Thank God for farts. I wished Paula could have farted."

The laughter from my mom's odd, yet sincere statement bubbled inside of me, just reaching my lips. Though it never broke the surface, I couldn't help but smile, and in that moment, I thought that somehow, someday, we might all be okay.

Acknowledgements

Thank you to:

April, Lance, and Stick for always taking my many calls and texts, praying for me, making me laugh, and talking me off the ledge over and over again. I literally wouldn't be here without you.

Angee and Charity for being the best sisters anyone could ask for. Your love and support carry me through.

Themba, my lifelong writing partner.

Casey, the first editor of every questionable thing I've written.

Jim, the father I wish I had. You've always cheered me on despite some really bad poetry. Your belief in me made me think that one day I might actually be a real writer.

Steve, for hosting our ragtag group of writers and encouraging us, in the nicest way possible, to just write!

The talented and generous *Rat's Ass Review* writers (particularly Vern, Jim, Meg, Ingrid, Robin, Sergio, Karlo, Mare, Jerry, Ruth, j ak, Munira, John, Hank, and Bob) for workshopping all the poems included in this memoir.

Kristin, Angela, and Alistair for being dear friends.

And last but never least, my children; Jazlyn, Jack, and Zipporah for living with a crazy mother and loving me in spite of it all. And to Sage, who's small, cute, clever, and not yet aware of my many flaws.

Love you all through the end of time.

MD Marcus currently lives in Raleigh, NC with two of her three children, a dog, and a bird. She writes of mental illness, motherhood, poverty, racial injustice, and the universal experience of love lost. In telling her stories, whether through poetry, essays, or her memoir, her hope is to make others feel less alone. Please pay a visit to mdmarcus.com to read more and to connect with her.

Publication acknowledgments:

I'm grateful to the editors of *Another Way Round, Communicators League, The Syzygy Poetry Journal, In-flight Literary Magazine, Femmewise Cat,* and please press where some of these poems appeared in other versions.

CPSIA information can be obtained
at www.ICGtesting.com
Printed in the USA
LVHW040746200421
684992LV00019B/1417